APPLE ACRE

Adrian Bell

Illustrated by
Richard Kennedy

LITTLE TOLLER BOOKS
an imprint of THE DOVECOTE PRESS

This paperback edition published in 2012 by
Little Toller Books
Stanbridge, Wimborne Minster, Dorset BH21 4JD
First published in 1942 by The Bodley Head

ISBN 978-1-908213-07-5

Text © The Estate of Adrian Bell 2012
Illustration © The Estate of Richard Kennedy 2012
Introduction © Anthea Bell 2012

Typeset in Monotype Sabon by Little Toller Books
Printed in Spain by GraphyCems, Navarra

All papers used by Little Toller Books and the Dovecote Press
are natural, recyclable products made from
wood grown in sustainable, well-managed forests

A CIP catalogue record for this book is available
from the British Library

1 3 5 7 9 8 6 4 2

CONTENTS

INTRODUCTION

Anthea Bell

AFTER HIS TRILOGY *Corduroy*, *Silver Ley* and *The Cherry Tree*, my father Adrian Bell's most successful book was *Apple Acre*, first published in 1942. That surprised him, for as he says in the Foreword (specially written, like the Epilogue, for the 1964 edition illustrated by Richard Kennedy, on which this new edition is based), he wrote it as 'a sort of diary at the ends of days'. His first publisher Richard Cobden-Sanderson had retired from publishing, the firm's back list had gone to The Bodley Head, and an editor there wrote to ask my father whether he was working on a new book. So he sent what he had. He comments in 1964, 'I still don't think of it as a book: it is just a picture of a hamlet of one hundred inhabitants going about its business in a war that changed the world.' That turned out to be its strength. *Corduroy*, an account of his time learning to farm in West Suffolk in the 1920s, had caught the spirit of an age already passing as he wrote it; in the twenty-first century it is social history, but the family archives contain letters on flimsy prison-camp forms from POWs in German and Italian camps during the war, telling my father how a copy of *Corduroy* brought England back to them. *Apple Acre*, in its own turn, conveyed the atmosphere of country life in wartime in the early 1940s.

My father was a diarist all his life. In our family we tend to adopt professions by accident, and although at the age of nineteen my father records his ambition to be a gardener and a poet, he became a farmer and an essayist instead, mining his diaries as source material for his essays. He was born in 1901, rather to his regret not quite in the Victorian age, and it was poor health that sent him to live an outdoor

life and learn farming. He suffered from recurrent, disabling migraines
for most of his life; the misery of one of them is recorded at the very
beginning of 'The earth crumbles' chapter of *Apple Acre*. We suspect
that they were caused by his difficult forceps delivery at birth. The
doctor thought the baby he had just brought into the world was dead,
and turned his attention to my grandmother; it was a sharp-eyed nurse
who saw a spark of life in the child. But for her, none of my father's
three children, six grandchildren and several great-grandchildren
would be here. For a man whose health was so frail, it was a good
span to live to seventy-nine, working to the end. He had contributed
a weekly column entitled 'A Countryman's Notebook' to the *Eastern
Daily Press* for thirty years, almost without a break; his last column
was written (and his last crossword puzzle for *The Times* compiled)
shortly before his final illness, and both were published just after his
death.

Apple Acre covers a year of country life in East Suffolk, to which we
had moved a few months before my brother and sister were born. Later
my father bought a run-down hundred-acre farm in the nearby village
of Weston, brought it back into good heart with some backing from
the War Agricultural Committee, and built up a herd of pedigree Red
Poll cows. The house with its large garden and orchard that appears in
Apple Acre was not itself a farmhouse, although we kept chickens there;
we lived in the former vicarage of the village of Redisham, Grunsham
in my father's lightly – very lightly – fictionalised version of it. I'm not
sure why he changed all names, particularly my mother's; here she
becomes Nora, in some of his other books Naomi, whereas she was
really Marjorie. He must just have thought that the initial N suited
her. 'Ada', who helped our mother in the house and was a great friend
to us in our childhood, was really Miriam and married to one of the
large village clan of Scarle brothers whose surname, to my ear, has a
Scandinavian ring to it. The area had been in the Danelaw; the nearby
market town of Beccles has many streets ending in the Scandinavian
suffix -gate, meaning road, and when my father sold the farm in 1949

to concentrate on his writing, the family home moved to Northgate there. But that was all in the future at the time of *Apple Acre*.

Once memory has set in it makes us what we are, and I don't think we ever feel very different. Leaving aside a few very early recollections, my own true, consecutive memory set in at the time when my father was writing this book. I remember the magic of that Christmas he describes when the doll's house arrived, and my equally magical fourth birthday – 'Anthea's best day – and the world's worst', as my father put it, for it was the day when Hitler's army attacked France and the Low Countries. It so happens that my own accidental profession has been as a literary translator from French and German, and in practising it I have often been brought to realise what a secure, protected childhood our parents somehow managed to give us at what must have been a desperately anxious time. When VE Day and the end of the war in Europe came, my father miraculously conjured up ice creams from somewhere for us three children; my contemporary, the Austrian author Christine Nöstlinger, describes in a book that is part novel, part memoir how at the same time her family was waiting in trepidation for the Red Army to march into Vienna. A close friend and her siblings were sent out of Nazi Germany on one of the last Kindertransport trains for Jewish children; their parents, unable to follow, perished in Auschwitz. It is humbling to remember how safe our parents made us feel in East Anglia.

As my father describes it, not much was heard of the war in our village except the sound of aircraft overhead (grown-ups could tell by the note of the engines whether an aircraft was 'one of ours' or 'one of theirs'). A small wood on my father's farm was cordoned off and had a notice planted inside it – Danger: Butterfly Bombs – when it seemed that some of these devices might have been dropped there and failed to explode. For greater safety in any air raids we children slept downstairs in the dining room, which had heavy wooden shutters at the windows, my brother and sister one each end of a bed along one wall, I in a bed along another and below a tall nineteenth-century wall mirror in a black and gilt frame, which came to my parents from my father's first publisher and his wife, Richard and Sally Cobden-Sanderson, who were also my godparents. The one really dramatic event was when the glass in the mirror cracked from side to side, like the Lady of Shalott's, not as the result of a curse but in a thunderstorm. That mirror now hangs on my own wall, and I regret the loss of the original glass: it was from the Cobden-Sandersons' Hammersmith house and before that, my parents said, from Richard's father Thomas, friend of William Morris and founder of the Doves Press. The old glass was dim and pitted with grey, but I imagine it in the past reflecting the face of Morris and other late associates of the Pre-Raphaelites. The wartime substitute is plain, without even a bevelled edge to it. In the present century, as my father predicted, pieces of family furniture still carry memories with them: my brother has in his house the solid oak table from a pub mentioned in *Apple Acre*, my sister and I each have one of our paternal grandmother's pretty Regency work tables.

At first glance *Apple Acre* seems to trace a full year in the life of the wartime village, from sugar beet harvest in one autumn to harvest festival in the next, but there is a long break in time in the middle. Once the Germans had occupied France, it looked as if they might invade England along its east coast, and my parents were advised to get us children out of the danger area. My mother took us to a picturesque but primitive cottage in Westmorland, and my father visited often enough to learn about north country farming on the fells of the Lake District; he wrote a book, *Sunrise to Sunset*, based on those months. There never was a Nazi invasion, we were back in Redisham next summer, so the closing chapters of *Apple Acre* belong to the latter months of that year, culminating in harvest festival in the little village church with its Norman porch and ancient carved pew ends in the choir (one, a bear's wooden head, had been worn half away by the touch of hands over the centuries). Our festivals were genuine celebrations of harvest, in which all offerings were the home-grown produce of farms or gardens. My father read the lessons in church, and the vicar, shared with our neighbouring parish, let him choose them. I thus first heard the magnificent language of the King James Bible resonantly delivered in that little church: the savage drama of the Old Testament stories, the gentler narrative of the New, the poetry of the Psalms, the Book of Job, Ecclesiastes – he picked all the best bits. Listening to him was an education in itself.

By the time the Westmorland interlude was over, as the latter part of *Apple Acre* shows, the twins could talk and I could read. I don't remember what it was like not to read, but I do remember learning. We used to exchange wartime parcels with Frank and Queenie Leavis, who were introduced to my parents by my father's cousin, one of Dr Leavis's students. (The great critic told my father that his books were naive, but 'naive in the right kind of way', which pleased him mightily). Sometimes a plucked and drawn chicken or other home produce made its way to Cambridge, and back came children's books for us from Mrs Leavis. She also sent the reading primer, illustrated by a family of matchstick men: 'Mr Peg is a man. He has a dog,' and so on. Once they can read, children with books in the house to a great extent teach themselves about the world, as I see my twin granddaughters doing now, and by the time the end of the war approached I was reading the newspaper. I knew very well that there was a war on, and I recollect seeing the photograph of Mussolini and his mistress hanging upside down after their execution by partisans. Country children are tough, and I was not so much shocked as interested; chickens with their necks wrung were hung in our larder just like that for a couple of days (the feathers then come out more easily). One thing did puzzle me, however: what could the newspapers possibly write about once the war was over? My mother, when asked, replied, 'The weather forecast.' It could not, of course, be printed in wartime for fear of giving aid to the enemy. I pictured – with some difficulty – column upon column of newsprint entirely devoted to the weather.

Not only was ours a secure childhood, in retrospect I see it as a privileged one. My father was an affable (and loquacious) man, genuinely interested in other people and what they did, as witness his accounts of the farmers and villagers in *Apple Acre*. He fell easily into conversation with anyone. Writers, moreover, were regarded as licensed eccentrics and didn't quite fit into any social class; as a result, we went to tea with the cowman's children and the children of the Lord Lieutenant of the county alike. It was not to the latter's house but another rather grand one that we were invited for a tea party, and my sister, still very small, was carried in by my father. Up in the air, she was level with the lavishly horned and antlered heads mounted as trophies on the wooden panelling. 'What for,' she inquired, 'are there goats on the wall?' What for indeed? We had goats at home, not just white Sally who arrives in *Apple Acre* (really Blossom, there he went again, renaming even the goat), but also two brown nanny goats, biblically named Rachel and Rebekah. Watching one of them give birth to twin kids was the best biology lesson I ever had. And surely my sister did well to associate horned heads with a useful domestic animal rather than big game laid low for the hunter's sole gratification.

This edition of *Apple Acre,* with illustrations by the late Richard Kennedy, was the brainchild of my former husband Antony Kamm. He was the editor at Brockhampton Press, the name of Hodder & Stoughton's imprint for young people in the 1960s, and he began a series of illustrated '20th Century Classics' suitable for young adults. Sad to say, Antony died early in 2011, but he knew that this new edition was coming, and liked the idea. Richard Kennedy went to see my parents, by then living in Beccles, looked at family photographs, and drove around to see the places that feature in the book. My brother and sister and I all consider that he caught the atmosphere of the time and place very well indeed.

So instead of exactly fulfilling his ambitions at nineteen, my father became a practising farmer (although he was always a good gardener as well), and the poetry went into his prose. I think, for instance, of his account of the coming of spring to Suffolk: 'In clearings there are encampments of primroses; great companies and rejoicings of them. The nightingales vibrate like light, the midday song of nightingales. . . . How could *The Pilgrim's Progress* have failed to be written in such a world? Think of this wood going on and on, covering the land, and at once it becomes more than wood – wonder and fear, the depth and mystery of the soul. The valley of the shadow: but the primrose is potent there: and in the deepest forests of thought nightingales sing at noon.'

Anthea Bell
Cambridge, 2012

FOREWORD

Adrian Bell

THIS BOOK is a picture of an English village in wartime. It was written in the early days of the war against Nazi Germany, before what Churchill called 'the end of the beginning', when the tide had not yet turned in our favour.

The village had not known an invader since the Normans. Previously the Danes had landed, and left Norse names which remain in the village to this day. For the village is less than ten miles from the East Coast. Later, the Normans came and built the toothed archway by which people enter the village church. Then, after a thousand years, a code word had gone out, which meant that a German invasion fleet was on the way.

The village waited. I remember the men standing at a crossroads with an assortment of shotguns, and an old farm wagon ready to be drawn athwart the roadway to make a road block. I wondered how many Germans armed with every modern weapon those shotguns and that old wagon would stop; but the men on that afternoon were more interested in the antics of a cock sparrow with his mate on a telegraph wire than in Hitler's tactics. Imagination just could not cope with the picture of an invasion after centuries of self-possessing peace. And the invasion after all did not happen. The village remained struggling with its old enemy and friend, the obdurate but rewarding clay, as it had been doing since Domesday.

But the village became aware of its new importance to the nation. There occurred (recurred, I should say, because it happened in 1914 too) overnight after the declaration of war, a reversal of the official indifference to the state of the soil or the solvency of farmers. I recall the first broadcast by the Minister of Agriculture. It was a call to everybody

who had a plot of earth. 'Dig for Victory' was the slogan. I was surprised
at how little cynicism there was in the reaction of farmers and workers
to the new summons, since I recalled very vividly the government's
shrugging off of the farmers' effort in the Kaiser war as soon as peace
was established, because that was when I had started to farm.

I had come to this village of Grunsham from West Suffolk just before
the Nazi war. I had a few acres here, and later, in 1943, I acquired more.
Our children were infants when the war started. Anthea was three, the
twins were only one. We were five miles from the nearest town, and had
no car nor petrol to get there. There was a bus twice a week. Otherwise
we relied on bicycles or a pony trap for our shoppings. We seldom left
the village in those years. There were shortages of the necessities of life
– of clothes, food, milk, eggs. We were lucky in having our own pig, our
own hens. Our staple food was potatoes and bacon. My wife made all
the children's clothes from old garments of hers or a store of material
we had laid in in August 1939. We had no piped water. Our well ran dry
regularly every summer: unless it rained, we could not have baths.

This concern for the home-grown and the home-made was one of the
conditions which gave a tone of emergency to the writing in this book.
It may seem a little unreal in these days of plenty twenty years after, but
it was a very real thing at the time. There is also to be reckoned with, in
reading this book today, the suddenly repentant attitude of the nation
towards its soil. Never again must agriculture be allowed to suffer from
neglect; never again must the nation forget what it owes to its farmers.
Propaganda sounded these notes continuously and successfully, as
recruitment to the Women's Land Army proved. I do not suggest that
the propaganda was insincere: it was deeply felt at the time. We were
fighting for our own land. The image in which we saw this England was
made up of its beauty, its fruitfulness and its traditions: it was typified
more by an old town like Lavenham than industrial Sheffield.

Rogation Sunday became known as Farm Sunday. The Land was the
subject of the talk after the nine o'clock news on that day. In 1944 I
was chosen to give this talk. The fact that the then Bishop of Lincoln

invited me to preach in Lincoln Cathedral as a result of it, shows how the nation's spirit and its agriculture were integrated at that time of stress.

To be found in possession of a pound of dairy butter was a crime. One of the first of the questions that our children asked was, what was a banana? They had never seen one. An undeclared sack of corn in one's possession was also a crime.

'Reconstruction' after the war was thought of in what would now be considered idealistically traditional terms. Men who waited to go into battle in tanks at Alamein dreamed of growing tomatoes in some sequestered English valley if they survived. Not only soldiers, but also women in the Land Army – our neighbour Brenda, for instance – dreamed such dreams. She had been a head buyer for a London store: she never went back to it. She bred pigs after the war and lived on a shoestring.

There was a league called 'A Kinship in Husbandry', which was formed, actually, just before the war. Its members included Lord Lymington, as he then was, Lord Northbourne, Edmund Blunden, Hennell the artist, H.J. Massingham the rural philosopher, also several clerics. Arthur Bryant took the chair at one of the meetings. We met in Oxford and London, at what Rolf Gardiner, a leading spirit among us, liked to call 'encounters', the idea being that views on England's future by so many minds from different angles but with an identical concern, must be cross-fertilising.

Our emphasis was on organic farming and living. We felt that a balanced life of people in an organic relationship to their home place was important. We envisaged, not a divorce between industry and agriculture so much as an integration of agriculture and light industry in what I now see was a too idealistic version of the part-time husbandman, such as the former village craftsman was, who also kept a cow, owned a pasture and a patch of corn. Nothing was left out: recreations – singing, dancing – were considered as a part of, not a relief from, the day's work. Folk dancing, it was insisted, was not a performance for the Albert Hall, but a thing of workaday meaning, a ritual just that much more elaborate than raising your hat or shaking hands, in the life of a people. Fire, by this token, meant something more than warmth, and water more than a piped convenience. Compost, of course, was a potent word among us; the utilisation of natural wastes. The basic premise of the Kinship in Husbandry was that man was plundering the earth's resources at a spendthrift rate and impoverishing posterity. This was before nuclear physics opened up a completely new reserve of energy.

So that was the Kinship in Husbandry. Today, with food production becoming more like a branch of big business year by year, that title may strike people as being of a piece with the Diggers and Levellers and other bodies of 'enthusiasts' in our island's history. But such was the mood of the times that it received under that title half a leader page in *The Observer* in the week of its inception. It followed the publication of Lord Lymington's book, *Famine in England*, which title, by 1940, almost qualified it to be suppressed as literature likely to cause alarm and dismay among the populace. That food was more likely to be scarce than plentiful now and in future, was the basic assumption of those days. Globally of course it remains true.

Of all of us, I think that only Rolf Gardiner continues to practise on his Dorset estate what was preached at those wartime 'encounters'. He relates downland to valley pastures for the rearing of hardy stock and the production of milk from them. He uses his own woods to provide timber for gates and fences, and also to supply an ancillary light industry (making brush handles etc.) on the spot. On Sundays his friends meet and sing in his big mill room at Springhead. They also dance the folk dances of a former peasantry for a continuing folk meaning in the twentieth century. Rolf is the one persistent David challenging the Goliath of industrialised food production. My own thoughts at the time were swayed not only by my love of the older order of farming, which was still the practical farming when I first went on to the land, but also by the fact that a director of an aircraft firm had told me that in his experience one hundred men was the optimum number working as a group for efficiency in making any product. Beyond that number he found that efficiency per man declined, he said, not only through physical, but also psychological factors.

This, then, is something of the spirit of the time in which I wrote this book. Occasionally a bomber would come down in flames near us, but for the most part the war was only a droning overhead. Mud and the weather were, as they had always been, the main adversaries in this remote parish. But I was too busy at the time really to sit down and write a book. I merely scribbled a sort of diary at the ends of days. This reposed for some time, a loose bundle, in a drawer. I only considered the possibility of its being publishable because the publisher who had taken over the stock of my former books from Cobden-Sanderson asked me, had I written anything lately, as he had not published a new book of mine yet? I remember I wrote, when I sent the script, 'I hardly think this is a book'. And I still don't think of it as a book: it is just a picture of a hamlet of one hundred inhabitants going about its business in a war that changed the world. The village has not changed even yet, except for piped water and some council houses, and a new pillar box with a wider mouth than the one that stood in the churchyard hedge and was covered with ivy so that it looked like part of the hedge. People are still nostalgic about the old pillar box.

So, when you read the following pages, remember clothing coupons, food rationing, and the fact that it was a crime to show the smallest chink of light from one's house or buildings after dark. But also bear in mind 'double summer time', in which six o'clock of a June morning was four o'clock by the sun, and we rose with the larks and the hares. You needed a permit to buy a tractor, but you could buy a horse without one. There were a good many horses still at work on the land of the parish. The life was a narrow round of days, but looking back on them and the straightforward tasks of farming and rearing a young family which filled them for us, I think that, but for the war, they could have been the happiest days of my life.

Adrian Bell
Suffolk, 1964

ONE

You would hardly notice it

ONE HAS PIGS and a little wood. Another has an orchard and fowls. Another is a wheelwright, with a vine growing up his workshop and a fig tree on his house. He also has four cows. Another has a horse, an ass, and (their offspring) a mule: with this team he ploughs an acre here, an acre there: on one acre he grew eighteen coombs of wheat. Another, old now, a wagoner in his day, has a double allotment on which he grows mangels, filling a hamper with them, harrowing them to the roadside where a farmer's cart collects them; forty hampers-full to a load.

Another has kept a family on 4½ acres.

Another who digs the graves tells of the multitudes buried in this earth. He knows the veins of soils, as he digs himself down out of sight into rock-like clay. Once, down there, he found the perfectly preserved body of a little girl.

The wheelwright's yard has flashing red ladders at harvest, while within a coffin is in preparation. It lies there like a person whom the wheelwright in his spectacles and with gentle hands is tending, filling every flaw in the clear flesh of planed wood. This to be lowered into the earth; the ladders to step strong men up to the tops of their stacks.

The corn stacks go up. 'Where's that thing for the bully-hole?' A niche halfway between unloader on wagon and stacker on stack, the bully-hole. A man stands in it like a statue in a façade, while the stack goes on building around and above him. The thing is found; a block of wood with three spikes to drive into the stack, the block for the man's feet. It came from the notably well-ordered little farm of a farmer now retired.

A young fellow, who was a boy at school the other day, now drives a tractor, standing up masterful, disdaining the seat.

There is a sale on Maypole Green. Was there ever a maypole? Sea-booted fishermen are there as well as an old clergyman in an Inverness cape. It is like an indoor sale, auctioneer and clerk sitting up on a table, people ranged below, only under no roof. For brief hours we are given a better opinion of our chattels. A cheap dinner service becomes 'nice old blue ware'. A tea service with a few blue blobs on it is 'Ah – very nice old Wedgwood style of thing'.

A man with dogs in a cart tries to sell a Dalmatian to the same crowd at the same time, to the exasperation of the porters ('Will you get your dog out of the way, please?'); then a pup held aloft ('Make a quid of him in London, easy'). Then he joins in the bidding for a gig, his horse and cart meanwhile straying away into a bog.

In the autumn the talk is of corn and potatoes. The church is full of sheaves. Then my daughter Anthea says that her fairy Rosebud puts on 'her frizzling dead-leaf shoes'.

At Christmas there is a carol service. Bob and Jim and Jeff and George swing two and two down the aisle, a light breeze in their surplices. Shepherd's sons, ploughman, stockman; they range themselves behind the girls in the choir stalls. Now one is Melchior, one Gaspar, one Balthazar. Out of their chests the bell-like voices break, powerful as their muscle with plough and iron. The girls answer, cool; and then all; 'Glorious now, behold —'

These are but a remnant: Joe is standing guard in khaki on the hill: others are all over the world. These light, white, airy capes are a remnant of whiteness in a world of khaki, a rallying-place of return, put on themselves now by men who hurdle sheep, manage horses, climb stacks.

In the inn the talk is of the tender mouths, the subtle noses of dogs; memories of muzzle-loading guns, of brewing, of curing bacon. The newspaper lies on the bar. It remains there folded all this Sunday noon, while dogs, guns, and how the old keeper used to brew —

In the spring the potato controversy breaks out afresh. In the first days after winter men stand looking at their empty ground and crying to one another, 'Epicure – you can't beat Epicure on this land.' Or, 'Majestic – I never grow anything but Majestic.' Suggesting that anyone who tries to grow anything other than Majestic (or Epicure) on this land is doomed to failure. Such words as 'mealy', 'waxy', 'watery', 'cook all to smash', fly about.

'Well, I *like* a waxy tater,' says another, and stamps off. And so on till the potatoes are all safely underground and beginning to sprout: then they become just 'my bit of taters'.

Our local merchant leans against a shop full of sacks of potatoes in the market town. He recommends every sort equally. A woman comes in and holds out three withered objects and demands to know what sort they are. The merchant glances at them with professional nonchalance, and pronounces them Sharpe's Express. They have done so well on her ground she will plant all Sharpe's Express.

But they are an early variety.

She will plant all early variety; why not?

'Well, you see, madam': the merchant's cigarette dangles between his lips and dances to his words: 'Come to the end of the season they'll start shooting.'

'I can rub the shoots off.'

'But they've lost their aroma —'

'Lost their what?'

'Their aroma: they've spent their strength' – the cigarette wags up and down, up and down – 'they've lost their virtue, madam.'

They look as though they have.

There is in this parish a wheelbarrow that is a hundred years old. It has had only the wheel renewed. It is at work for the fourth generation. Its owner says it is the best-balanced wheelbarrow he has ever handled: the handles are curved in such a way, and where you grip them, they are so thin that a child could grasp them. The weight is all on the wheel. It was the work of a local man.

There is a well at one end of the village which produces a reddish-brown water which has been pronounced officially to be non-poisonous. There is a pond at the other end about which no official opinion has been expressed. These are the drinking supply.

Electricity passes through the village; but none of the cottagers can afford to have it. There is no post office, school, parish hall. Every cottage in the village, save about three, has been condemned. Two of them have, in addition, been empty awhile. A cheerful villager has just bought one and hung a bright green iron gate.

Sometimes you move a heavy stone and are surprised to see creatures living a hidden life underneath it, some small irregularity in the under-surface of the mass holding off its weight and giving them a home. So under the weight of mass-legislation an unregarded but persistent local life goes on. It is not recorded in forms, it cannot be seen by the visitant or passer-by. As to this village – if you drove a car from the town situated five miles on one side of it to the town situated five miles on the other side, you would say, 'We passed a house here and there, yes, but there was no village.'

TWO

Leaves in the furrows

THIS IS THE LAST HARVEST, the sugar beet harvest. It is too late for a harvest really: the potatoes are up and the mangels clamped, the stubbles ploughed. Yet this last crop is ungathered. At least it is a fine start, a crisp wind and sunlight that makes the farmhouses stand out naive and clear, as in a child's picture. The lifter draws easily through the earth, which is dry and crumbly, and we who follow, clad in aprons of sacking, knocking the roots together and scattering the earth off them, agree that it might 'do' much worse. Of course nobody will admit to there being any pleasure in sugar beet lifting ever – only under certain conditions it is more supportable than under others. The position is back-breaking, and the grit that flies off the roots impedes conversation: if you open your mouth too wide it flies in. But conversational it is, of course, like every other field operation; only when one comes on a beet that the horse-drawn lifter has missed, conversation is interrupted by a grunt and a 'blast'.

'I don't mind as long as the weather's fine,' old Mr Winch beside me says. 'But if it turns wet I shan't come no more. I'm not forced to do this, you understand.' Mr Winch is proud of his independence, and who wouldn't be, at the age of seventy-three, to be able to retire from farming seventy acres to a neat cottage and live on his means?

In actual fact the whole of his retirement consists in that one phrase, 'I'm not forced to do this'. To occupy in the evening of life a theoretical easy chair is the proof of his success as a farmer; so he is keen to remind you of it, though actually he is working as hard as any of us in the field. I don't know quite why he comes to work; is it to oblige his former neighbour, Mr Camm, on whose field he is working; or is it to be in sight of his old farm still? Those fields which contain his life fascinate him, and he is followed out here each day by his white cat, who also has a strong homing instinct. Every morning, 'Here comes Dick Whittington,' says one of Mr Camm's young labourers as the pair arrive. The cat sits under the shelter of a beet plant most of the day, with an occasional prowl round.

Then after we have lifted a good many rows of beet and flung them on heaps, we take special little billhooks and scrape more earth off them and cut the tops off, and make a heap of the roots and another of the tops.

All the while we stand each at our heaps, we talk. There is no sense of being static; we seem to be travelling through the day. It is, I think, due in part to the brisk-moving broken sky; in part to the high ground on which we work with a view of the road and other farms and their work. By dinnertime the carts are going to and fro to the road with cleaned beet; we load them with big, blunt-pronged forks; the young labourers are quick and strong at it. The few last beet of a heap are teasing to pick up – one flings down his fork impatiently and takes them up in his hands.

Mr Winch and I sit and have our dinner on a bank beside a pond on the border of this farm and his. We talk of what is before us – food, field paths, the pond. There is a half-rotted plank over the ditch and the remains of a stile can be seen in the hedge, overgrown and almost hidden. 'There's not many people in the village know of that path now,' Mr Winch says, 'but once it used to be a lot used – before bicycles.' He traces the course of the path to me – how it leaves the road just opposite the Barley Mow that used to be. The pub is no more – only an iron bracket on the wall of a house shows where the sign used to hang. Thence, the path skirted fields (paths seldom cross fields in this arable country), ran round the big wood, came to the brook, followed it right through the grounds of The Hall, passing within a hundred yards of the mansion itself, and so by devious ways to another road within sight of the market town. I think, while he tells me this, that though the word democracy does a lot of work just now, that derelict path was an artery of something more than departmental government allows us today – for every Tom, Dick and Harry had been able to walk past the squire's coverts and through his grounds for centuries, and successive landlords either would not or could not close the path. And other paths Mr Winch speaks of, saying that he could get up from this spot and walk to the sea without going on a highway at all, except to cross it. These tracks were much used, he remembers, for smuggling. There were few farmhouses hereabout that did not have their supply of smuggled tobacco and spirits. Only last year Mr Brett and his men were demolishing a condemned house when he fell right through the floor – a brick floor laid apparently on solid earth. Underneath they found a beautifully built little vault of brick arches and one or two old barrels – alas, empty.

'But I never drank spirits – though I could have had plenty, cheap. Home-brewed beer – all the years I was in Magpie Farm I was never without home-brewed beer and home-made bread. And I do wholly miss 'em. We haven't got the conveniences where we live now – and the missis, like me, is getting old.' It is odd to hear him classing as conveniences the bakehouse with its brick oven and brewing copper at Magpie Farm, whereas his present house contains more of what are usually meant by that term today.

The pond at our feet, one of those sudden, small, and bottomless-looking Suffolk ponds that occur in out-of-the-way corners – that has a memory, too, a tragic one. 'That's where poor old Jimmy Trousler —' Mr Wisden now appears (he comes out and works in the sugar beet field after dinner). 'Remember poor old Jimmy Trousler?'

'Ah – he drowned himself in this pond,' says Mr Wisden. 'Left his stick lying up against that todd tree. This is it.'

'Yes – that's it.' The very stick that Mr Wisden is carrying apparently.

'I wonder what he did that for —' still looking at the stick as though it were a clue. 'I was thinking of he the other day,' says Mr Winch. 'Now I've no farming to think of I often cast back in my mind, sitting at home. Jimmy and me, I remember us sliding on this pond in the winter when we were boys.'

'He hadn't no missis,' says Mr Wisden who also is a bachelor – 'he hadn't no worries that I know of. Booze as much as he liked.'

'Ah,' assents Mr Winch.

'The best man with a stallion that ever travelled along these roads.'

'Ah – that big Suffolk stallion of Lord Petter's he went with. I was in Stambury market that day when he was arrested. There he stood drunk with the horse at the crossroads. They arrested him because they said he weren't fit to have control of a stallion. They took him off to the lock-up. But then nobody couldn't move the stallion. So they had to fetch him out to take it away. Another day, the policeman finds Jimmy lying drunk under the stallion by the roadside; but he dursn't arrest him because the stallion wouldn't let him come near him. That horse was proper fond of he.'

Then Mr Prinker comes along and we start work again. He has twenty pigs and a nut wood; and has just been stood off from a big estate near by. The estate had to pay £40,000 in death duties when the landlord was killed in the service of his country in the last war. His son is fighting in this war. Crushing war taxation has meant the dismissal of twelve of the estate workmen – all skilled men, who kept the farms repaired and the woods a model of forestry. Mr Prinker vouches for the story that one of the men dropped an empty cigarette packet in the wood and the master saw it and made the man go back and pick it up.

'I've worked fifteen years on the estate, and I've never heard him raise his voice to a man. But if he thought you'd been long enough on a job he'd come and shift you on to another, or tell you to start on something else next week – you knew then without any telling that he thought it was about time that job you were on was done.'

As we go up and down the rows discussing the war – 'I know what I'd do to Hitler and Goebbles and his lot (whanging a Hitler beet against a Goebbels beet till the earth flies like shrapnel), I'd —' But then a drove of bombers and fighters go over, and the men stand a moment, and a different, deeper feeling comes over them about the war. 'Such a thing never ought to be.' This is beyond a flesh-and-blood anger.

Now again talking of the estate; Mr Prinker has stories to tell of meticulousness of management, of care of buildings, of hedges, of cottages, water supply; until you realise that the man has no deeper loyalty in him than to that organism, and not through any abject dependence, but simply and solely for it being run in a way that satisfies his fundamental feelings about his surroundings. By that token he feels the master as a person to be trusted in all his dealings, even in making Prinker redundant (through the agent). It is not he who has done it, but this catastrophe. And in that context the war is in the character of

Fate, to which the banging of two beet together, as also the speeches of politicians, are irrelevant.

He loves his nut wood, indeed, and his pigs, but the impending loss of the latter is only a personal matter, in which he can feel aggrieved and angry at what he considers official short-sightedness; and anger – whether against a personal Hitler or an English official – is a relief.

'Have you ever seen a pig crack a nut and eat it?' he asked me once. He assured me that a pig could do so and eat just the kernel and leave the shell. I was rather disbelieving until that autumn we went gathering nuts in his wood and came upon the pigs there and saw them actually picking up fallen nuts, cracking them in their jaws, and letting the fragments of shell go; eating only the kernel. They do it so neatly. Pigs are in their element roaming such a wood, and Mr Prinker has been a sort of pig-centre for the village. He supplied cottagers with single pigs from his litters, and his pigs were always hardy and thriving on account of being woodland-bred. At one time he used to be an unofficial pork butcher, killing a pig occasionally and selling it in the village; in fact the village hardly relied on bacon from outside at all. There was no need to – the people cured their own, and you could not get better pork for curing than from Mr Prinker's pigs. But latterly the whole subject of pigs has become hedged round with so many restrictions, particularly difficult for people unused to the written word and unused to writing (for them words without the sound of the voice and its inflexions are almost meaningless; hence the reputation for stupidity), that it has become a matter of fattening and selling *en bloc*. Now feeding stuffs are dwindling; Mr Prinker is distracted by the sight and sound of hungry pigs. 'I can't stand it,' he says. 'I shan't have no more.'

'I never did like this bought food – you don't know what's in it.' And then as we reach the ends of our rows and straighten our backs and face each other – all this time we have been talking to beet plants – 'I believe,' says Mr Prinker, facing to the sun, 'in home-fed pork. I mean barley like I used to buy off Mr Camm – and then you've got something that'll stand up to your knife.'

'Victuals,' murmurs Mr Wisden as though to himself, standing chopping the top off beet after beet. The juicy crunch of the knife through the beet, and the dropping of the top back to earth. 'The pulp'll come back, too, and that'll make dung. This old field needs feeding after a crop like this. Twelve men stood off did you say, Mr Prinker? All repairs stopped to farms?'

A storm blows up suddenly – a spring-like storm. We shelter where we can. Winch and Prinker have disappeared into the farther ditch; I find the girth of the todd tree friendly – the one that Jimmy Trousler leaned his stick against before plunging into the pond. The many-coloured landscape has turned grey and seems all bowed away from the wind. The young labourers crouch under the cart; the white cat under a beet plant. Only the horse and Mr Wisden have no shelter. He just wraps his dun-coloured coat around him and turns away from the pelting shower, patiently letting it beat on him, as the horse does.

Waiting for the storm to spend itself I think of that fine estate and its beautiful woods, and of its owner who was killed in the last war, who filled his park with trees, of his son who has cared for those trees, of the great walled vegetable garden with its wistaria arbour that is a kind of Eden. It is only to pavement minds that such things are class-war themes; the peasant does not envy, he understands them. His own cottage garden is based on that red-walled acre; it, too, has its arbour. The same standards govern the great place and the small. I am cheered by the tenacity with which these countrymen cling to the values of things when the things themselves are lost. That phrase about meat standing up to your knife, for instance; a whole rule of husbandry is hidden in it. And Mr Prinker's pleasure in watching a pig crack a nut.

After harvest I started to break new ground. It was hard, the grass summer-thick and upstanding. Great mats of it I pared off and laid face-down in the trench, and then the dark brown earth that dug out in squares, just like a diagram of how to dig in a gardening book.

Anthea used to stand and watch in her summer frock; she immediately recognised the brown squares my spade cut out as chocolate cake. Such a profusion of chocolate cake, there was one for everybody; Father, Mummy, Anthea, the babies, Grandfather, Grandmother, Ada. All the dolls had one each, even the dog and the two cats. Still more and more chocolate cake. We had to rack our brains at every spadeful, casting around for relatives and friends, till even imaginary people had to come and receive them.

'And whose chocolate cake is that?'

I paused and wiped my brow. The day was hot and golden, with a cooling stream of air among the trees, which occasionally dipped and touched the grass. I had on my old summer shoes that creaked because they were broken in the middle. It was my foot as much as anything that held them together; they had grown used to my feet. I looked at them and remembered wearing them for the first time. Flowery May on a holiday in the West Country: an inn where Nora and I had stopped for bread and cheese and cider, kept by a Cornishwoman and her husband. He had been huntsman to a Devon pack: he looked like a huntsman still. At half past five one cubbing morning, she told us, he had said to her on a hill, 'What's so good in life as this?'

The tables in the inn tap room were scrubbed bright as new breadcrust. Our prismy glass mugs of cider stood up like solid gold. Outside there was a little garden and a yard of fowls. The yard seemed to expect horses: the cobbles, the rings let into the wall, the mounting block.

Afterwards we walked by the deserted canal and the swirling river. After living so long in Suffolk the differences of the west – the rocks, the rushing streams, and above all the cold stone echo, made it unreal yet more than real, like a dream.

That evening as we limped tired and happy down into Bath, which lay in its hill-bowl as in some blue fluid, the shoes made themselves felt. The steep downhill was worse than uphill; there is something about the inability to brace the knees that makes one laugh. We had to stop every now and then, seeing Bath still a long way beneath us. Every time I lifted my feet the shoes, the then new shoes, discovered tender places. But I would not mind feeling those pains again, to stumble down that hill again, in an England at peace again, to a city that beautifies, and does not befoul, its countryside.

Now there is no other pang to be had from the shoes; they have fitted themselves to my feet. Now they are thoroughly decayed, bald, and the stitches all frayed out. It is doubtful if they will see another summer. They lie mildewing in a shed.

The first rain came – too early – and the digging was taken over by a pair of big black boots. They clanged down upon the spade; a heavy unhandy spade that had broken the poor old shoes just under the instep. It finished them, trying to break new ground.

Still it dug well – better really for a little softening. Moist rather heavy days; apples shining boldly in the trees. Anthea came in her mackintosh to look for worms. They were wonderful to her, suddenly showing pink and naked against the turned earth, then their slow elastic disappearance.

'Where's that worm going?'

'Into its house.'

'What sort of a house?'

Describe a worm's house. Ever let the fancy roam.

'I think it's going shopping,' Anthea says. 'It's going to buy some cheese; it carries its basket on its tail.'

Digging is quite a complex process really. A fairly powerful machine would be needed to turn earth to the depth of a spade. As for trenching it – when it is a matter of breaking up the subsoil you get into the realm of great agricultural engines, to do on a large scale (and rather clumsily) what the spade does so neatly.

The spade is the microcosm of husbandry; and when you get spade multiplied by spade. A man I know used to be employed at an institution where they had five acres of vegetable ground. This he and five other men used to dig together. They started in rotation, as men do who set out to scythe a field, and when they were all going they got into a swing which carried them on, so they talked and worked together all the day, and in the evening they had the satisfaction of seeing a big piece dug, denied to the solitary digger. 'Those acres grew for everlasting of stuff,' said the man.

Then the institution got rid of the men and bought a little one-horse plough that only scratched over the surface of the ground, and they couldn't grow anything.

One day as Anthea was watching me dig she had the idea that she must feed her children on this rich stuff, this chocolate earth. The dolls were all upstairs, but she brought half a dozen stones as proxy. 'These are my pretend children.' That was all right, but there weren't quite enough, so the old kitchen spoon used for the feeding had to be the pretend seventh – Topsy. The difficulty arose when it came to 'pretend' Topsy's turn to be fed. How to feed pretend Topsy with pretend Topsy? Anthea was not long at a loss. One of the stones – pretend Susie by name – had to deputise; pretend Susie became pretend pretend Topsy and so released the spoon. It seemed quite simple and natural to Anthea and only took a moment to arrange.

Then the rains came in earnest. Day and night followed day and night. There was no more drying after that. The trench became full of water. It stayed full; it started an aquatic life of its own. Frogs found it a long, long swim. Some even died there. Leaves made a black, rotting floor to it. Every time I passed it on my way to feed the animals, I looked sadly at the pale belly of a dead frog looming through a stagnant scum, and thought of summer and tea under the oak in haytime. My spade as I had left it one evening ready to start again standing in the trench, rusty, blade-high in water. I took it out, dried it, and put it away.

Nothing more could be done unless the water could be got away.

When you begin to look at a level field with a view to getting the water off it, it suddenly ceases to be level. It lifts a little here, dips a little there. That deep boundary ditch becomes a thing difficult to reach. To get a furrow from this trench to that ditch, falling all the time. It is done at last, but still it takes only half the water, a slight depression at this end holds it up. By taking out a whole spit more at the ditch end, it is

possible to deepen the furrow through the depression by a few inches. A little worn spade does this last spit, narrower than the other, sharpening to the edge. When this spade bites the last bit of earth between the furrow and the trench, all the water in it that has lain stagnant for weeks suddenly wakes up and goes slipping away.

Then a bright morning and the spade is brought out, the clumsy digging spade. The rust is soon gone: the dead frog disappears for ever under a spit of earth. Under the grass, now flat and matted wet, the earth is still dry, chocolate-caky; but I am alone now: it is too cold for Anthea to stand. I hear her starting off for a walk with Nora and the twins. It is winter now; the trees are bare. It is dark at four. It will soon be Christmas. 'You can dig what you like before Christmas, but after Christmas it don't do to touch this heavy land.' I dig and dig, for Christmas is coming. I look up occasionally to see the sky reddening. A pink cloud over the oak looks calm as I toil. Sky reddening, fowls walking up their plank to roost. On and on. I reach the boundary line.

At last it is done; a clean trench, a straight edge. I clean my fork and spade in almost dark, cleaning fork on spade, then spade on fork. Our squat house is a black silhouette against the sunset sky. A thrush is singing far off. I sit on a log by the woodpile under the oak and unclog my boots slowly, with a rotten stick that breaks and breaks till I am almost doing it with my thumb, too lazy to look for another. The air is frosty, but I have enough heat from my work to make it pleasant to sit here, tired, by the bare earth.

Seven-fifteen: it is a bitter dark day. For five minutes I lie awake, feeling the tug of lethargy; not mere laziness, but a vast cosmic lethargy, as of all the hibernating creatures and all the leafless trees. But hens do not hibernate: I hear the crow of a cockerel. Then I remember those dawns I should not have seen but for the animals to be fed, and climb out.

A splash – it is a little splash – in cold water makes a difference.

My scythe hibernates by the window in the shed, and its blade curves right across the view of the orchard through the old leaded panes. There is something pleasant about that view of the orchard as I mix the meal – cobwebbed, softened at the edges with winter jasmine, a few of whose yellow stars have already burst out, and the strong tapering shape of the scythe blade stretching across it. A composite memory of flowers and fruit and labour. Apple boughs cross it too: the apples are in open boxes here, the nearest dusty on top with the meal. Yellow-red, rather soft apples; then some green ones that turn golden after Christmas, and will keep till spring.

The wife of a village man said, coming out of her hot kitchen one hot day, 'Oh, I should like a nice English apple now!' She had no more thought of her wish being granted than if she had asked (he said) for a bottle of champagne. 'But I said to her, "I believe you shall have one." I remembered what I'd forgotten for months, a box of apples I had laid in my gig house, meaning to take to a friend. I hadn't gone after all, and there those apples lay, as sound as on the day I put them there. My wife was thunderstruck when I brought her one. That was the first day of June.'

I do not remember how the man's miraculous escape from a shell in the last war came into the apple story, but I can still see the little leap he gave, demonstrating it; and knowing the way of country stories, have no doubt that there was some valid connexion between the two.

In another box are the little russet apples, so small and so sweet, that took such a long time to pick.

On the other wall hangs the old flail, that was made by the grandfather of my old ploughman. Its parts had once grown in the hedge. Staring at it as I mix the meal, I don't think the flail looks as though it has gone up on that nail for good: no, it hasn't that look about it somehow. Perhaps boy Martin as an elderly man will be using it some day on the farther side of civilisation, saying to his son, 'This, my boy, is a relic of the time before the machines; before my father's time, that is. Lucky there were a few of these left for us to go by.'

The meal is mixed; I go out into the yard with it. There, through the kitchen window Nora is already having her steam bath of dishing out the porridge. The light is on: it has become a shock to see a brightly lit, uncurtained window. But officially the blackout has been over for five minutes. Going out into the field I am faced with a greater brightness, a dawn of rolling fiery clouds, and underneath it all a jet of real wild fire. It is William's bonfire of hedge cuttings, leaping to meet the conflagration of the sky; the two identical in colour. It is difficult to believe they are not vitally connected, but merely together through an angle of vision. Vision anyhow it might easily be interpreted, with William's body silhouetted against his fire, a little black twig of energy, struggling between darkness and day.

Toad-in-the-hole for dinner; a good dinner for a raw day in November less than ten miles from the East Coast. My belly is comforted. Passing Mr Barron's holding I stop in the east wind to let Mr Barron's son pass, who comes riding out of his gate on a cycle, dangling a dead rat on a piece of string.

'They're worth tuppence now,' he cries as he pedals off, 'and tuppence is worth running about after these days.'

It is ten days ago now since I met Mrs Barron escorted by what seemed all the village children with their hoops, soapbox chariots, whatever they had in hand when the old lady set out. This troop of children, when not at school, is always waiting to follow anyone who looks as though they are on an interesting errand. They wait for Mrs Brett at milking time, then all come home with the red cows in a little festival.

For some days the children have been acting as scouts for Mrs Barron's lost cat. Two had just brought news of its being seen in the vicinity of my place; so freshly as to bring Mrs Barron out – a rare thing. They wandered up and down the road once or twice, and then stopped and became a sort of deputation at my gate. Mrs Barron made her request: if I had seen that cat, or should see it —? With so many apologies for bothering me; but it was such a special cat, had never strayed before, been gone now several days. Had it been an ordinary cat she would not have dreamed of troubling me — I promised lookout for the cat, for which I was thanked as much as if I had already discovered it.

I gathered little about Mrs Barron's cat but that it had a white front. A white-fronted cat, image of my white-fronted kitten, has appeared from time to time, glared wildly, and fled at sight of me. Would that, I ask Mr Barron, be his cat? Ah, no, they know that cat – no, theirs is more of a Cyprus cat, as you might say. He wouldn't mind if only he knew what had become of it. The affection for the cat is deep. 'I've never had a rat about my place till just lately: why, I've known him sit all night on the neat-house roof waiting for a rat.'

'This war – ah, that's a bad business. Nobody can tell what's coming. We can only pray to God.'

'Come and see my pigs: I've just whitewashed all the places inside.'

First a path scraped of mud, then a door and a long narrow aisle with a glimpse of grass at the other end. On either side pig pens built of hedge poles, young trees, variously boarded; all a whitewashed dimness, and the white pigs inside looking anything but white; pink and butter-coloured rather, among clean straw. The place looks to have grown as much as to have been built. A gale is blowing down the passage, but the toad-in-the-hole is still with me, and I wear two jackets, an old and an older one. As we stand talking – 'You see there's just the old-age pension, so one wants to do something. Besides, I've never been used to sitting about. The pigs keep me well: I'm over seventy. I've swung a scythe from five in the morning to seven at night in my time, like my father did. We sold £140 worth of pigs from here last year. My wife keeps account of everything in a book. If we was to make but a shilling profit on each sovereign's worth – well, that's something. Then there's the fowls in the orchard, too.'

Just then the son returns with the twopence for the rat which he offers to his father who refuses it. 'Go on, that was your rat,' says the son. 'Go on, you killed it.' 'No, that's yours.'

A sow is to be let out on to the little plat of grass while her sty is re-littered. 'Ready?' 'Let her come then.' She comes trotting along the dim tunnel-way towards the grass: she fits it like a bullet a gunbarrel.

'That was nothing only old bog grass when we came here.' (In the spring, now, it comes up like a lawn, thick and shining.) 'That's the pigs doing. I don't cut it: they eat it all down.'

A thing I like to stop and look at in the spring is that plat of grass, so thriving, responding so vigorously to the sun.

The sow is called back: she comes sidling along the chicken wire. Another little lawn there. 'Before we wired that in, the old sow she would meddle with the chicken coops. One day she got one stuck on her head. What a sight, her running about with that on her head, bumping into everything! A job I had to get it off. At last I managed to get on to the coop: I sat on it, and called to my missis to bring the saw.

'This butter rationing: if I had a bit more meadow I'd get a cow. But it's no good having one cow: you must have two.'

The grocer's van draws up by the yard. Eyeing the van – 'They say, how did the chaps have the strength to do the work they did in the old days, with so little money to live on? My father, do you know, when he was sixteen he weighed sixteen stone. He got into a good farm. If you could eat fat bacon, there was as much of that as you liked, and flat cheese and beer and skimmed milk – not separated mind, just once-skimmed. If you could get into a good old farmhouse. But I mustn't keep you standing in the cold . . .'

Inside, in the dim whiteness, the ting of pails on troughs, squeals of pigs and slop-slop of those feeding. Late afternoon village sound, sort of curfew of November.

Outside, the shed is black-tarred and abuts on the road. Visitors see only the black blot of a shed, hear the noise, and smell the smell. 'A very piggy corner of the village that. Pooh!'

Turning into my own gate I glance at the left-hand paddock, too often hayed. That it could ever come to look like Mr Barron's. Put pigs in it? Pleasant to loiter for ten minutes, too late to do anything more now but watch a small rift of red where the sun is setting, and wait for the fowls to go to roost, and think of the pigs. A portable shelter? I look indoors. Grandfather is blacking-out, Anthea running to and fro telling an excited story, while Nora is getting tea ready. Anthea gets tied up with her words, and looks as if she is going to burst. I speak about the pigs.

'They'd run off with the portable shelters,' Nora says, 'and arrive, shelters and all, at the back door in the end.' Everything comes to the back door, cats, hens, calves when they break out; and so would the pigs. They are safer, perhaps, in their brushwood sty.

I go out again: hens at roost, still murmuring, pigs deep in their straw. I pick three roses – memory of summer – and gather some oak twigs for my fire; close the hen house, go indoors. The kitchen and scullery seem full of people: washing being damped down and rolled into a sausage, kettles steaming, cups clattering. A mass of dark-red and yellow chrysanthemums in a bucket, picked for fear of frost.

Filling being put into a new cake. Anthea has got on to a chair see.

'I want a piece.' Occasionally she tries something quite obviously unpermissible. 'I want a piece now.' 'Whoever heard of such a thing!' It has worked: she begins her chuckle. 'I want a piece now.'

Taking off my boots, feeling warm and cheerful beside the

chrysanthemums, I begin, 'Do you know, when Father was a little boy —'
That always makes Anthea look. 'Yes?'

'— When Father was a little boy he always had to have two slices of
bread and butter before he was allowed to have a piece of cake.'

'Yes. And did your mummy make you a chocolate cake, with fillin' in
it?'

'No, it was just a plain sponge cake: (I do remember a lot of that plain
sponge cake) and no filling in it.'

'Yes.' A small voice. I look up sharply. The head is lowered, the face red. The thought of Father getting only plain sponge after the dutiful two slices is almost too much.

I hasten to add, 'But if he had been a good boy he used to have a chocolate biscuit sometimes.'

'Yes.' A whisper.

'But then,' crescendo, 'when it was his birthday he used to have a lovely cake, all sugar icing, and Happy Returns of the Day written in pink, and candles —'

'Yes.' The head higher.

'And he used to have lots of little boys to tea with him, and they played all sorts of games.' A smile.

'Why, look at pussy – she's trying to catch her tail.' She is having a whirling fit on the floor. Relief and joy.

After tea I take the three roses and oak twigs into my room. I have just put them on the mantelpiece when all the lights go out. Soon the house is peopled by candles and assumes an air of vigil. I light the two candles on my mantelpiece in the old wooden sticks. I blow up my fire, putting on the twigs. It flickers on the walls: there is a mingling of lights. Some of the twigs have leaves on them, dry but greenish still. I look at the shape of the leaves in the candlelight. I cannot burn them. Something long forgotten has reawakened out of the shapes of the oak leaves. Alone in the soul of a room I hang the oak leaves on the picture above the mantelpiece.

The light cut off, civilisation cut off, leaving me alone in firelight with three roses, some oak leaves, and the wind in the chimney.

THREE

Ankle-deep and axle-deep

A ND STILL the sugar beet are not all lifted; and still Mr Winch comes daily, or on such days as any of us come, when it does not pour all day. Looking at the field now it is impossible to believe in that fine start and the earth powdering off the beet. All is mud now. Little Mr Winch, immersed in it, looks a dwarf. Yet he comes every day well provided, with a piece of clean dry sacking for apron, and two other pieces to wrap round his legs. Sometimes he changes these at dinnertime for another set he has stowed away. 'I do detest mud,' he says more than once. I know he means it, yet think it odd that a man should farm successfully on some of the heaviest land of Suffolk for two generations and then say that. But on reflection it does not seem so odd, rather the mark of the good farmer; for what is mud but earth misused? His former neighbours have told me, 'Yes, Mr Winch, when he had Magpie Farm, would always be out with his scraper in the winter in his yard. He couldn't bear a lot of mud about.' His gateways were made firm with pounded brick. He pulled and shaved the sides of his stacks: a tidy farmer.

'Mind you,' he says to me as we straighten our aching backs a minute to look at the storm clouds, 'this is a good farm of Mr Camm's, but I wouldn't live up here for anything.' It has an old plaster and tiled house right away by itself in the fields, among its buildings and paddocks full of stock. An agent out to sell the farm would describe it as approached by a good private road. It is good as far as it goes, which is roughly halfway. When we started the sugar beet the whole road was as hard and smooth as the highway. By now the second half, which has no bottom of stones, is a mire. Wheel tracks diverge from the main track, and other tracks from those tracks, in an attempt to find a bit of solid ground; so the road becomes a sweep many yards wide. There is a shed at the end of the stone road, and that is the depot for all goods in the winter. Yesterday an unwary lorry tried to go through, and where it plunged in and was finally extricated is now a fair-sized pond formed by broken land drains, which one of the young labourers is today trying to unblock. It makes a desperate-looking mess, his digging among ruts and water. 'No, that would drive me mad to live up here,' Mr Winch says.

Mr Camm is used to it. He took his farm for a lifetime, and has put a great deal into the land; yet could not bring himself somehow to spend a lot of money just on stones for the road, preferring to get used to winter isolation. And his wife is quite used to the routine of setting out on foot in gumboots, and changing into shoes at the shed, and getting into the little car for market. Mrs Camm is the embodiment of good management, neat, compact. In fact, expressing like one of her husband's round stacks solid goodness and nothing wasted.

There is nothing to choose between this and Magpie Farm for goodness, yet to Mr Winch the one is a home, the other anathema.

'I'm glad this isn't my field,' he says, as the loaded cart goes lurching off, bogged to the axle in the struggle roadward. Standing loading the beet we found ourselves stuck: we had to down our forks and pull on our gumboots, or we should have left them behind. This we had to do at every heap. The field is spouting water from broken drains everywhere. The beet lifter will no longer work; it merely anchors the horses. We have to lift the beet by hand entirely, levering them out with a two-pronged sort of fork – a laborious business.

It is an orgy of mud. No good waiting; the beet all have to be in by Christmas, and it will not get any drier till next spring. To stand in one place for ten minutes is to take root. Birds look incredibly light and free.

'I shan't come no more; it's getting too bad,' Mr Winch says. 'I'm not out to get the rheumatism. I'm getting old: I shall sit back now for the rest of the winter.'

All day it is the story of his farm just over there. Every field that he tells of is in view: a fascinating story. Yesterday, it was how he had to

buy or quit after the last war. He bought. The price was high: it was like starting all over again. This morning it was how his wife saved the farm one critical year with her fowls. Now he is telling me how his son one day ploughed two acres with a colt that was difficult to break in, using the other two horses in relays.

'But he wanted to get on to this mechanised work,' he added.

The present owner of Magpie Farm is a young man from overseas. Mr Winch suspends judgment; but he looks anxiously in that direction. He has not seen the mud scraper at work yet.

'This machinery,' he says, puzzled, 'was to save labour. But my son Tom works twice as hard as ever I did.'

I, too, have seen Tom on some contract job of cultivating, lurching and bumping over a field of clods on his tractor, from dawn till dusk, and after.

'Sometimes he comes home too tired to eat, too tired to sleep: he's so stiff the wife has to rub him with oil. What sort of a life is that for a man? Why should a man work like that?'

Indeed, the inexorable activity of the machine seems to have entered into his blood. I can hardly think of him as a being alone, in silent air: the motor din has become his aura. I never see him out of the seat of his machine, except for certain curiously quiet days when he is doing swift repairs. He is successful with the machine: the standard is, 'keep her running'. Even before the emergency of war the price of the machinery made that imperative.

But today I think of a different Tom, in the light of the story his father has just told me of the colt. Tom on the two-horse farm ('The boy always was a worker'), Tom determined to master the horse, breaking it to the plough. The father's bewilderment: 'Machinery should *save* labour.'

How peaceable and smiling appears his lifetime of hard-hand labour on Magpie Farm by contrast. I, too, feel happy in the mud here trying to slice the top off a beet with one chop, without wasting any of the beet – by no means easy: trying to scrape off the glutinous mud, thinking, that's good earth to be washed down a factory drain. I hate to think of it going down the factory drain, when it ought to be fostering barley seed here next spring – if ever the field can be reconditioned by then.

But I am wistful over Magpie Farm. I know every field of it by now: I feel as though I have worked for a lifetime beside Mr Winch on it. I should like to take Magpie Farm and work it in the way he worked it. What has happened to that colt, I wonder, which promised so well? One of his cows I know Mr Cardwell has: he stood in a gale to buy it. Gale or no gale, bidding was keen for it: the cow was well known. He continues to praise it. Oh, I should like to carry on Magpie Farm now, before there is a possibility of it becoming a lesser thing than it was.

Another storm. We shelter as we can; but the hedges are thin now. 'No, I shan't come no more,' Mr Winch says, unwrapping his sacking. He emerges surprisingly neat and clean, and mounts his bicycle. There is a tone of finality in his words this time. I think the story of Magpie Farm is over.

I am teaching Anthea the days of the week. 'What is it today? What is it after Friday?'

'Why,' she cries, 'you know what it is today – it's party day.'

Which is true. There is a children's party at the Hall; she has not forgotten.

It is sunny and frosty. It occurs to me that Nora is having an even more thorough turn-out than usual of the bedroom. Bump, bump, bump. Really, what is she up to? Then I realise it is not Nora but guns. Outside, these deep bubbles of sound burst in the clear air and make the windows rattle. There, across the sky, lies as it were a long bar of pure white cloud, spreading at its base and thinning out into a curly mesh. It vanishes to a point in the north. It lies there in the blue, calm as a feather, while another series of thuds shakes the house.

That is all. Anthea meets me again. She says, 'I've been readin' a picture in a book, about a wolf who says "I'll huff and I'll puff and I'll blow your house down."'

'Shall we go for a walk, Anthea? I want to see Mr Brett.'

'Yes,' running off. 'Mummy, please put on my hat and coat quickly.'

Out on the road Anthea looks back. 'What long shadows we've got. My shadow looks like a big girl: and there is yours.' Pause for the contemplation of shadows. She tries to unstick her feet from her shadow and finds she cannot.

We meet two little boys near the village shop. 'Hello, Anthea, we're rich; we've got one, two, three half-crowns. I know a boy who goes to our school: he's ever so rich, he's got twelve and sixpence,' says Simon.

Only a penny is actually in evidence, which they take into the shop, whose bow window has a red paper chain draped across it. They are too excited today even to follow us. I am quite thankful, because they have large sticks with which they do war dances, flinging them to and fro like javelins, to everybody's danger.

As we walk along Anthea speculates on the party. 'I wonder who will eat the quickest?'

'I expect Ralph will. Little boys often do.'

'No, I think I will. I'll race at eating.'

Knowing Anthea's habit of reverie, slice in hand, I think it extremely unlikely.

'We mustn't be late,' she says. And then, as though fearing to get too far from home on party day, she stops. 'Now we'll go back.'

However, I persuade her as far as Mr Brett's. Mr Brett is busy rebuilding the front of his workshop. I ask him about some hay he is going to cart for me; then we talk of bricks, of the old local bricks, dug from those spots hereabout that are now ponds. 'The old people got very clever at burning them.' These bricks are as much local materials as plaster and beams. Perhaps that is why on these winter afternoons a haze seems to rise from the newly-ploughed earth and claim the old red-brick cottages as part of itself. Each, as dusk falls, seems to acquire the character of the other: brick-colour deepens, earth glows.

The different kinds of bricks: those big, variously-shaped flooring bricks, called 'grass bricks', very hard, and with the pattern of grass impressed on them. Because, Mr Brett thinks, they were laid on the grass

to dry. He shows me one: there is a curious beauty about the fresh shapes of growing grass there on the face of the brick, a pressure of the past.

This workshop used to be a cottage. It is tiny, yet it used to be a double cottage. A family of seven sons lived in one end. 'The youngest of them,' says Mr Brett, 'will be ninety in January.'

I approached Mr Brett's yard as he went to show me the grass brick; Anthea mutely resistant. All this talk of bricks. As we move on, she says to me, 'I believe you've made us late for dinner – stoppin' there all that time.'

After dinner, about three o'clock, Anthea and Nora appear dressed to go out. Nora in the green suit, five years old, but so manipulated as to the skirt, whose length and shape have been cleverly altered, as to look quite new. Anthea is stiff under the spell of a new coat. But outside she remembers the party again and sets off at a little trot.

I follow an hour later, after feeding the animals. The cold is intense: a rime is forming on everything. Of all the population of the hedges, only a solitary blackbird and a wisp of old-man's-beard remain. Yet there is something exceedingly beautiful about this walk between flat meadows and ploughland in winter dusk. The way the white ducks of the farm sit placid in the grass, while a few fowls are roosting in a tree, heavy shapeless blobs against the sky. The pond is ice, its verge is scored where horses have slipped. Manure heaps are steaming, cattle stand like monuments.

I enter the park, and the trees make a maze of bare boughs meeting above, through which a star seems to precede me like a needlepoint going through lace. I slacken my pace for the sheer variety of the boughs; ever some new curve. Beneath the bridge the stream runs under a lip of ice, and makes a loud tinkle among the motionless trees.

The Hall is blacked-out so thoroughly that approaching it through the silent park is like coming to a deserted house in a fairy tale. Not a sound, not a soul, not a glimmer. Only the red sunset bars in the west, and a star – Venus – bright and low.

Suddenly then I burst into a room glowing and scintillating with candles, with children in bright frocks like flowers, sitting round a long table. The wave of warmth, the brightness, the rosy children eating cakes and pulling crackers, is like a fairy-tale transformation indeed. Long and long the old Hall has stood empty, winter after winter. So recently has it become a home again that one half expected to find only darkness, cold, and a scuttling rat.

The fairy godmother of it all greets me, while small hands continue to help themselves from the plate in her hand. I am so stiffened with the cold walk that my face muscles will not work, and my mind also is paralysed by the shock of brightness, so I can say hardly a word. A

chair and a cup of tea and a plate of jam sandwiches are before me: jam sandwiches, thin and patchy, with the jam soaking through: I have not had such since I was a child myself. I eat all the jam sandwiches. There is Anthea, solemn with enjoyment, her hair golden in the light. All the children sitting round; the strange child-quiet, staring. This sitting round of children before candles is somehow out of time, eternal.

I find myself next to two mothers, and catch on to their conversation. It is of how to keep their fowls now there is so little corn. We discuss potato peelings, old crusts, cheese rinds.

Another father arrives; he is in khaki. Everybody is moving into another room for the Christmas tree. Parents congregate. 'Did you see that aeroplane brought down this morning?'

'Was it brought down? I'm glad: I only saw the smoke.'

'It went straight up into the air, then down.'

'Like a towering pheasant.'

'I'm told it came down in the sea.'

This goes on over the heads of the children. Their eyes are fixed on the coloured lights: small hands move with determination towards various objectives. Anthea stretches for Ralph's drum: Geraldine's arm crosses hers and extracts the blue teapot from her doll's tea set. Anthea gently but firmly reclaims the teapot, and puts it back in the box. She puts the lid on. She tries to hold it high above everybody's head. 'In case it gets broken.' An auburn-haired girl comes to the rescue and holds it safely, being the tallest, and takes Anthea by the hand.

At last it is time to go. All the children have their coats and hats on. Anthea stands in the hall with auburn-haired Janet. 'Anthea says she is going home with Janet.' We laugh. But out there in the hall Anthea is perfectly solemn. She stands in her coat and gaiters holding Janet's hand and facing the big door, waiting for it to be opened. She has formed in an hour such a perfect speechless friendship with Janet that she would walk straight out into the night with her anywhere.

* * *

In church this morning there were chrysanthemums – deep honey-coloured chrysanthemums. Outside misty thaw: here chrysanthemums and four candle flames made a warm glow. Just a handful of people today: the psalms and hymns were all harmonium. A kind of ghost of a service: the robust old words of the Reformation sounding on mostly to children. The boy behind me spluttering and coughing, 'And our mouth shall show forth Thy praise.'

Yet what it must have been when the villagers brought their flute and fiddle, and the pews were full. What it might be – but it is no good blaming the people; you must blame industrialism that has rotted the old forms and put nothing in their place.

When you listen to the words of the old collects and prayers and blessings – stout-hearted, no sentimental cringing about them – the tiny handful of you on a dark winter day in the little church in the fields, and you cast your mind to and fro across the present world with its great hide of armour plate, and receive its embattled neo-paleolithic stare – you know then that there is nothing, absolutely nothing left, no integrating atom, but this small church in the fields where the old blessings are still pronounced, and four candle flames conspire with chrysanthemums to make a glow of faith.

As we were lifting sugar beet the man beside me said, 'Do you know if it's today they're burying Tim Dukes? Because I'd go to the church if that be so, as him and me were mates; we worked together.'

It happened he had been buried the day before. But it would have been fitting for his mate to have walked in straight out of the beet field, with muddy buskins.

Dukes hailed me one day as I was passing, seeming to burst his small casement window out with his body wedged in it. 'Hey, sir, just a minute, sir, if you don't mind.'

So I went up the garden path and he led me into his room with a 'Come in, sir, please sit down.' The room was crowded, because his wife's bed was in a corner; she was half paralysed by a recent stroke and could not get upstairs. She wept for a minute with sheer vexation and despair that she could not do the things she wanted to do. 'Don't you mind her, sir, she do feel it, having been a active woman all her life. There now, don't you take on so.'

There I sat, plunged into the daily life of the ageing labourer and his wife, a thing which I almost *felt* in the air, by the shadowiness of the room and the crowd of chattels, a few old simple pieces polished with use and handed down; a beautiful old chair to which he had botched a new and staring leg, things of use, and an odd assortment of decorated biscuit tins and seaside ornaments. And the iron bed in one corner, taking up a third of the room, and the maimed woman, her worried-looking hair, and her husband, his face rather like a gleam of sun, his voice hard with the out-of-doors, his whole body and movement too big for this cave of a room. It was one of three cottages: the other two were empty and tumbledown. The two did not seem so much to be living here as to be confined here, caged-in.

Dukes was pouring me out a whole tumblerful of raspberry wine with which to drink to Christmas, and I drank it all down, while the woman wept again at something her husband had said, stirring a recollection of herself when she had command of her body. What it meant I well understood; and why her nerves were like a bolting horse; because it was not just a matter of resigning herself to being waited on; who would there be to do the waiting? For the time her husband made shift.

But she did not only cry: next minute she laughed, telling a story against herself; how our place had stood empty once for a long time, and the village being very badly off for water she had gone up there and found the well full of water. Only it was not the drinking water well but the dead-well into which she had let down her bucket; rain water running through had cleared it. Her husband discovered her mistake in time.

Dukes meanwhile showed me mementoes of former masters. One a red Paisley handkerchief of great size. Another thing was a cup and saucer handed down, china that shadowed against your hand. I could guess how it must have been prized when wooden trenchers and earthenware mugs were the cottage utensils.

Dukes was out of a job, and he seemed cut off from the village and the fields, sitting there staring out of the window.

Outside he opened the door of his shed and it was lined with implements, all the blades of husbandry; billhooks, reaphooks, slashers, blades of varying and subtle curves. All these tools were polished and greased; I should not think there was a speck of rust on one. King of all was a heavy cavalry sabre which Dukes took down and drew from its sheath, shining like new and the blade murderously sharp.

'I got it at a sale,' he said. 'I thought it might come in handy for a rough old hedge.'

Someone to whom I mentioned this array of tools said, 'Tim Dukes, he always was a one to have the right tool for a job.' An expert hedger, he goes down as. There, too, was his bicycle; old but as polished as the rest. The opening of the door of that shed was a revelation after the rather haphazard room, and the ruinous state of the cottages. It was like a glimpse of culture. I thought with shame of the state of my own sheds.

I met him one day later near the pub. I was glad of the opportunity to invite him to have a drink with me. He had on a new pair of gloves. He offered me a hand like iron, like a claw. He had a pair of these gloves every year; the gauntlets reached halfway up his forearm. He had thick buskins on too; he was armed against all hedges. But he had no hedging to do. He was over seventy, though he did not look it.

His voice seemed to have receded into him, deep down, when I met him again. He had had an attack of some kind, which the doctor had told him was nerves. A strange diagnosis, I thought. He woke in the night and found he could not move. He had just got out again; his former corn-coloured complexion looked leaden and he complained of a constriction in his chest. But he had dug his garden. He had taken days over it, resting every quarter of an hour.

When I saw him again (he spent much of his time now leaning on his garden gate) he said, 'I've been worrying, that's the trouble. I can't help being worried, no use pretending I can.'

It was not difficult to see what he was worrying about. He and his wife were now equal to about half an active person between them.

Dukes died quite soon after that. His wife still lives on in the cottage. Another woman of the village – one of the busiest – goes and sees to her every day; takes her to see her husband's grave, gives her dinner at her house. Yesterday she was sawing up wood for her in her garden, a bough of that old apple tree of which Dukes said to me, 'That's a King Pippin, that never did bear; but then I dug a trench all round it and emptied my closet pail into it. After that we had lovely apples.'

It is just a year ago I passed him cutting a roadside hedge. I think it was the last job he did. Going down that road yesterday I saw the cuts he had made, clean, no slivering, and thought of the greased hooks hung up, and Tim Dukes in his grave.

FOUR

Christmas candles

'YOU CAN'T CALL THAT AN ORCHARD,' my mother said, on a visit to us, as I used that word referring to the meadow in front. She did not think much of my home; I don't know why, for it is convenient and stoutly built. To her artist's eye it lacks something. I am not sure how many trees a meadow must have in it to merit the name of orchard. I suppose I had been seeing more in it than there were; I had seen my intention of trees. In the same way country people will refer to a grove of trees long since felled. 'Down by the willows.' You may look in vain for the willows.

To have an acre of kitchen garden surrounded by a red brick wall: that is a thing I dream about, but shall never have, because with it go always a mansion and park. My other ambition, to plant an orchard, I have now begun to realise. I have never planted fruit trees before; only bushes, and they do not count. When I say plant an orchard I mean an orchard of standard trees on proper trunks that will live for a century. There are always so many arguments against standard trees, when it comes to the point. It has always been, 'Bushes are cheaper, are easier to control; the fruit is more easily picked,' and so on. So it has been bushes: but I never felt like calling that an orchard. It had no longevity in it to my eye.

But here I have an unanswerable argument in favour of standard trees – they will allow of stock grazing the meadow beneath. And I am here, I hope, for life. So it was with real pleasure I ordered standard trees.

And here they are, embedded in an enormous bundle of Norfolk reeds.

I do not know what machine-age meanness it is that makes one think that six shillings is a lot of money to spend on an apple tree. I blush to think of the number of times I have spent that on some manufactured thing, and thought nothing of it. But for a fruit tree to live in one's view for life – There is a popular feeling that something that has grown should be almost a gift, has cost nothing; I don't know why.

It is only the beginning of an orchard. I have learnt, at last, to begin slowly. I am not so old but I shall pick plenty of fruit from my trees, and still leave tons and tons for my children and grandchildren.

It is a mild, sunny day. William and I set to work. I have marked out the places with sticks. We plant as we dig, knowing better than to dig all the holes first and then come and find we have ponds to plant in. I profit by William's experience on this land. He planted some apple trees years back, and they have never grown and never borne. This is dour soil for fruit; heavy and wet. Yet, as I told him, I have walked through Herefordshire orchards in the spring, when at every step the turf sank down like a sponge and the water came up to one's ankles. Yet their trees bear. Anyhow, we plant very shallow, each tree in a couple of barrow-loads of compost earth wheeled from my manure heaps; residue of burnings, trimmings, ditchings and muckings-out.

We have just got the first tree planted when the air raid siren sounds from the town. No noise could be more eloquent of mechanical death: it seems to grip life by the throat and congeal the free wind. The tree stands slim and insouciant in the din, the sun glinting on its clean bark. There is Time hidden in a young tree; it has a look of tomorrow. William's hat on a stake is twisting and turning.

'I think that's a pretty noise,' Anthea says, cocking her ear as she comes out to me with her little trowel. 'I'm goin' to help you, so I've brought my travel. Where shall I dig?'

'You dig here,' I tell her, as I firm the earth round the tree while William is digging another hole.

'I *do* like helpin' you plant trees,' she says, scattering a few ceremonial grains of earth round the trunk. 'When I've daggen this, then where shall I dig? And what are you doin'?'

'I'm cutting this old stump down, dear, so I can plant another tree in its place.' One has to squat at it half sideways: the sappy wood grips the saw. Orange-coloured particles fall on a cushion of moss.

'When will it fall down?'

'Soon.'

'What are you stoppin' for?'

I (puffed): 'To have a rest.'

'When will it fall down?'

'In a minute now.'

'You must saw it off soon, because then I want to see you saw another tree down.'

They must be well staked. Only yesterday I came across two iron rods that had once supported a curtain. I thought, as I shifted them from one corner of the shed to another – as one does, thinking that is tidying up – 'These, I suppose, will lie about here for years.' And today I have found a use for them, to stake two apple trees.

Then we hear the guns. Dull and sullen, they sound all the afternoon, while we plant trees in the sun. Nora takes the children to the post, walking slowly along the sunlit road in the boom of the guns.

William has a way with tools. I had a pair of clippers, but they are lost. They will turn up in a manure heap. Then an old knife which I tried to revive, sharpening it on a stone of Nora's little rock garden. A real rock garden, not a slag and brick one. Nora's is an ecclesiastical rock garden, full of sculpt fragments. I am sure in the beginning the churchyard must have been plundered for it. Ferns grow out of broken oriels; sea pinks couch in ogees. Some day I shall find a noseless angel among the primroses.

I never lose faith that I can revive an old blade, patiently honing it on steps and stones as I go about. Sometimes it seems to get sharper; then again blunter. William's tools are always sharp; they are worn fine and sharp; they never have that stubborn appearance of a new blade, thick-looking.

William has a way of tying a tree to its stake so that it does not rub, making a stiff little arm of twisted cord between them. An affair of many twists and knacks of the fingers.

'Of course, I reckon half-standards would do best on this land,' William says.

I don't care: I want trees that the next generation will have to take a ladder to. And they will have to learn the management of ladders: how to foot them round and coax them deep into a tree without breaking the branches. And how to carry a forty-staver in a wind, making a pause between lifting on the shoulder and starting to walk, to get the balance of it. And how to carry a ladder up a ladder, when you want to mend a roof. In fact, the whole art of the management of ladders, about which a book could be written.

I am not afraid that my trees will not grow. I have a feeling that I can make them grow. There they are now planted, and the moon is up. Their first evening in the orchard. They look beautiful among the few old trees. Yes, I *can* call that an orchard.

'A hurdle, quick!' I cried, as the pigs came scampering into the backyard, against all the rules. Such things will happen. We penned them in a corner, caught them (ear-splittingly), and returned them to their brushwood hovel. What a handy bit of fencing a hurdle is. How we should miss it in a host of ways. Farmers who lightly talk of sheep wire and electric fencing as complete substitutes – what but a hurdle, I should like to ask them, will make a pig go where it does not want to? Two or three people with one each make a sort of travelling pen round him. And to pen a calf up from its mother in a corner, or stop a gap in the fence temporarily; why, I should be lost without hurdles. But they melt away – old sows have powerful snouts; calves grow strong and jump. And other people's cattle break down your stop-gap.

The hurdle-maker's is a happy sort of place. Late in October, when I went there to order more hurdles, he was trimming up stakes. He has great cone-shaped piles of poles standing on end round old trees, dwarfing his house. He has a yard and a range of buildings. From one of these buildings came drip, drip, drip. 'The last oozings, hours by hours.' The smell of apples was mingled with that of wood. Within was his cider press; his father's and grandfather's it had been. Sacks of apples lay about, and a tub full of brown apple mush. People bring their apples, and he makes them into cider for them, as well as his own, and fills their casks. Through the gate I could see his orchard, with hens walking about it. Cider-making is not a business with him: he crushes other people's apples to oblige them. It used to be a business when he was a boy. His father and grandfather used to put the press on a cart every autumn and go the round of the district making cider from people's orchards. 'We used to sleep rough, as they say; in barns, on hay or straw. I used to love it. Oh, I looked forward to October.' I could imagine what fun it must have been to the boy, sleeping on the hay or straw high up in some barn, with an outlook in the morning through a knothole of a new countryside. Every day somewhere different. The men, too, enjoyed it, the sociability, the bit of roving; dragging their old wooden press about on a cart like a rough-hewn Bacchus. 'It was as good as a holiday.'

One could visualise the preparation, the setting off, the return; all the homely touches. But it is over now. I still wonder what is the secret of the inertia that has paralysed the country in all its workings. A little thing like this matter of the travelling cider press: was there any reason why it should not have continued? It interfered with no trade. Commercial cider in bottles? But the old cider drinkers do not drink that. 'I had two glasses,' said the cider-hurdle-maker; 'it went down very cool, and when you've said that you've said all. Why, if that had been two glasses of my old cider —'

The old cider drinkers must have died out. Last summer I saw the tractor driver tipping up a bottle of raspberry-coloured-ade delivered by a lorry, and another lemon-coloured bottle by his dinner basket. It is curious how these little pockets of cider-making and cider drinking occur in our barleycorn East Anglia.

Numbers of wooden casks of all sizes lay about the shed waiting to be filled. Meanwhile the hurdle-maker went on with his trimming of stakes.

Yesterday I was there again; and now his yard is full of new hurdles, glittering with them; and he has orders for many more. Others crafts have died, but his remains. He enumerated to me the country tradesmen in this one locality when he was young: wheelwrights, blacksmiths; builders' yards and painters' shops. Usually two or three would be contiguous, their work being complementary. I should have passed, on my way here, at least three such settlements, with their masters and apprentices, working up the timber of the woods all around. A tumbledown shed, an open space, marked these places: I noted them as I went back.

A big park was about to have a complete new fence – a mile and a half of it – of rived oak. 'I knew the man that rived the old one, that was forty-five years ago. He rived the whole of it, from oaks out of the woods.'

A hurdle is the sort of thing I could have learned to make. My reputation as a handyman has always suffered from the fact that my work is more durable than showy. I have made efficient hen coops and sawing horses. My family once made a sawing horse: not a bad piece of work, but I had to brace it. I set up an arch for roses. The others envisaged some piece of neat dovetailing I should execute and creosote. I searched about and found a bough roughly the shape of an enormous reaphook and affixed this with a minimum of hammering. It was at first derided as an evasion of the job; but as time goes on everybody comes to see the beauty of my natural arch and the interest of its unsymmetrical curve.

I should like to have been a hurdle-maker. You work in the woods in winter: you bring home a great store of ash poles and set them up round convenient trees, wigwam fashion. And in summer you sit at home in your orchard making your hurdles. I should say it is a task which has that repetitiveness which avoids monotony, because no hurdle can be exactly like another, any more than one sheep can. I wonder at what stage in the making of a hurdle a man becomes aware, 'This is going to be an extra good hurdle', because perhaps the wood's slight vagaries fall out conformable to the shape of the structure or the grain is particularly clean and straight? In another life I'll be a hurdle-maker with an apple orchard, like the one I have known, with a cider mill in which to crush the crop and make cider. The riving of ash and the dripping of apple juice went well together, I thought, when I called on him. And with a few fowls to peck around and pause and watch you work, I should say it could be a happy life to a man of sound ambition.

I have a demi john of cider left, old, deep as sunset. I had it from a friend who has a hundred acres and a mill and a cider press on the Suffolk border. He grinds his own corn in the mill, and makes his own cider in the press. He and his wife can never drink all he makes before another brew is ready; so it gets older and older.

I go to seek it in my cellar, for this is Christmas Eve. I pass three withered, arthritic-looking legs sitting on the stairs. They are stuffed with little presents. Nora creeps into the children's room and fastens them in place.

Anthea is the presiding genius of this Christmas. Father Christmas is instinctively comprehended (after all, what more credible than a jolly old man distributing toys all round?). Moreover, she has seen him, as she will tell you. It is true: I saw him myself. In the town market square, while a small, glittering snow sifted down, he came in a cart drawn by what looked like a reindeer. (At least it had reindeer's antlers. They reminded me of a pair on our doctor's wall: Father Christmas had much his figure) – followed by children singing carols, flanked by swinging lanterns, round and round the great twinkling Christmas tree standing in the square. Snow on the roofs all round, and old windows glowing. There was a spirit abroad that night; something lovely that had lived in this land raised its head. But the children departed, and traffic flowed again and white headlamps broke through. Still, after that who could doubt? I did not even myself. That was the last Christmas before war.

The twins are not old enough yet to understand about Father Christmas. Not for want of Anthea telling. Loudly telling.

Christmas had become a feverish effort to boost up trade, those last years. Its lovely spirit was lost with commercial Father Christmases standing in muddy gutters. Trust money making to pick up a bit of old legend and put it in the cash register. Christmas morning came to have a relapsed feeling, a thank-God-the-shopping's-over feeling, a view of shuttered shops in the mind's eye.

And now. Yesterday afternoon I sat and listened to the singing of carols from King's College Chapel. I saw in my mind again that building which I can never approach without being filled with a sense of life. And the singing was like the foundation stone of a new England.

This morning I go to drink the health of some friends. The children are absorbed in their stocking presents (though still Martin's old rag doll is the favourite plaything), Nora in the preparation of the Christmas dinner. I explain to the lady of the house that the hour of our drinking together here is the most critical in the cooking of the dinner, so Nora could not come. I find myself deep in conversation to right and left, till I notice that people are thinning out, and take my leave. I am in that careless mood in which one reaches for the first coat one sees and has forgotten the way out. As I cycle off I recollect the acceptance of an invitation from my host to go on the river with him in his boat and fish. As I know nothing of fishing there seems something a little curious about it, it being winter.

Perhaps we are to sit wrapped in old coats waiting for pike.

The cockerel I killed for Christmas weighed 7¼lbs., and along with home-cured Bath chap, sausages, stuffing, and that old cider of Suffolk, makes a glorious meal. The plum pudding is good, too; but not quite equal to one we ate last year which was two years old. My friends of the morning are having a goose from the farm opposite their house. There were a dozen of these geese, and it was a pleasant sight to see them walking out every morning in single file. As Christmas approached the procession dwindled till there were only two left. Then one. Every morning they saw the goose destined for their own table walk out alone. And now they are eating it – a little sadly.

We too have tried keeping geese. Every countryman some time in his life keeps geese. Usually once is enough. I have observed the sequence. Retirement to the country. The making of a tennis lawn. Effort of harrowing tons of earth for levelling inflames the sciatic nerve. 'O Lor' – the lawn needs cutting again. 'Wet season; six mowings to one game of tennis. Incipient despair. Enter boisterously cheerful friend. 'My dear fellow, all you need is half a dozen geese.'

We too tried geese. Our problem was the orchard. I put my cow in it, but she browsed on apple buds. I put goats in it, and they only wanted to eat apple bark. Hens made holes in it and engendered nettles where no nettles had been. Pigs ploughed it. But no beast would harmlessly graze it. A friend said, 'Try geese.'

Nora and I were cycling one day when we passed a small farm where a board was nailed to a willow tree, and roughly scrawled on it in tar were the words, 'Goslings for Sale'. We dismounted. The yard was empty save for a corn drill with two old boots under it. Suddenly the boots moved, and there emerged from under the drill a man. Goslings? Yes, actually they were his boy's, he said. He walked with a stooping, lolloping gait to a straw yard. He opened a gate which fell to pieces in his hand. He put it together again and led us on. His boots sank into a brown ooze. 'It's all right if you keep to the edge,' he said. We followed him, hanging on to posts and nails in the wall. Something heaved itself up out of the straw on the opposite side of the yard. It was a bull.

I scrambled into the shed whose hatch door the farmer held open, pushing Nora before me. We were in darkness. 'There they are,' said the man. 'Over there.' I could hear a hissing, snuffling noise. 'They're half a crown,' said the man; 'a month old.' 'We'd like six,' I said; and turned to go out. But the bull was looking in at us over the hatch door. The bull blew froth from his lips. The farmer waved at the bull. 'Goo on, Jack Johnson,' he cried, and prodded him gently with a stick. Jack Johnson blinked and walked backwards. The farmer opened the hatch door. We came out and walked backwards from the bull. 'He'll not interfere with you,' said the man. He had put six goslings in our basket in the twilight of the shed. Nora was charmed with them. 'They look just like pussy willow.' We paid the farmer fifteen shillings. He saw us off at the gate. He pulled the notice off the willow and affixed it to the gate post, fishing a bent nail from his pocket, and using a flintstone as a hammer. 'What did the boy want to go and nail it into that tree for?' he muttered. 'The seed of that willow came in a load of marsh hay; that were the last load my father carted.' He seemed to value the tree on that account.

'Got a bit behind with things,' he said, submerging himself again under the drill.

We cycled home carefully with our treasure of goslings. We spent a long time mixing them food, and erecting a shelter for them, and laying bricks round their coop to keep out rats, and constructing a wire front. Next day there was a thunderstorm. Nora suddenly cried out, 'The goslings are all dead.' I rushed out. They lay on their backs in the rough grass with their feet in the air. We picked them up, wrapped them in flannel, and laid them in a box on the edge of the stove. They revived.

Every time a storm blew up we rushed out. Sometimes they were already on their backs as though dead. Sometimes we caught them before they had succumbed.

They were voracious. 'Of course, later on,' we said, 'they'll live on just the grass.' Meanwhile we plied them with messes of boiled wheat and barley meal, maize meal and oats. Soon, we thought, they will begin eating the grass. But they did no more than toy with the grass, poking about in it in a disgruntled sort of way. As soon as we appeared they came at us hissing for more barley meal. We referred to a book and read, 'Goslings require very little artificial food, as they consume large quantities of grass.' I wished these goslings could read.

We withheld the meal for a day or two, but the honking and hissing and gaggling was more than we could bear – and the sight of the six lined up at the gate, surging to right and to left as we moved to and fro in the garden. Their tactics were intimidation: they even hissed at the hand that fed them.

And then one day towards Michaelmas, they happened to be at the far side of the orchard when I went out with their food. They stretched their necks and came full pelt – full waddle, that is – their wings flapping. Suddenly the leading goose became airborne, and then the others. Their feet continued paddling the air. My impression was that they were as surprised as I was to find themselves flying. They gathered momentum, overshot the food, gave one despairing honk at it, and sailed out of sight over the hedge.

I went indoors. 'Our birds have flown,' I said to Nora. 'What – the geese? I didn't know they could fly.' 'Nor did they, I think. But come to think of it, wild geese fly, so I suppose tame geese can.'

'Nobody told us that. Does one have to chase one's geese about the parish like a swarm of bees?'

I walked in the direction in which the geese had disappeared. I came to the farm whence we had bought them as goslings. It was not far over the fields. Mr Grimm, the farmer, was ploughing with a pair of horses.

'You looking for your geese?' he cried. He pointed to his unkempt hedge. 'They've got themselves in a rare muddle.'

There they hung among the thorns, some upside down, some spreadeagled, some vertical. They must have hit it in full flight.

Mr Grimm left his plough and helped me extricate them.

'They don't half look comical,' he chuckled. 'Thought they'd come home, I reckon. As a matter of fact,' he added,' I could do with some more for stock.'

Torn and bleeding, I sold them back to him there and then. I went home and got out my scythe. The orchard was more difficult to mow since the geese had trampled it. But I didn't care.

While the children are playing we get busy with the Christmas tree; the same that was given Anthea for her first Christmas. I dig it up again from the garden, with all the earth on its roots, moist, to keep it alive. I like the earth to come in, too: I hate the idea of the trade Christmas tree chopped off from its roots. Some yew also and trails of periwinkle leaves and ivy. And somebody has gathered a bowl of real summer roses.

It is a nice matter to balance the candles in their holders on the little boughs. There is still a blob of spilt wax from last year, blue, which an elderly lady botanist stooped to examine with great interest last summer.

What innumerable hiding places there must be in a house of children. Presents have been concealed this last fortnight in my room, under my carved oak table (carved with farm men's names: it came out of an inn), on top of my bookshelf. I am looking for *Rural Rides* and come across a set of doll's furniture. And I forget the book, remembering the cold shop, and the woman in the back room turned temporary showroom, sharing a meal with a blue cat in a basket chair by the fire. And in the very cold front shop, the proprietor blowing up a football for a boy and looking like an old picture of Boreas.

The Christmas cake also comes out of some secret place. There is a present also for Mummy from Anthea, chosen by Anthea at my suggestion in the shop, then this morning wrapped up by us together, and a suitable message written by Anthea's (guided) hand. And Anthea then running off to the kitchen. 'Mummy, we've got a secret for you.'

The great thing is a doll's house which Grandma has bought for Anthea. It is a bright, garden-cityish sort of doll's house, with diamond-paned windows that open. It stands beside the Christmas tree, and the sprays of yew are to it as might be trees of its garden.

We bring in the candlesticks for the table, and by the time the children arrive the candles are lit. Anthea comes in and stands bathed in delight, her hand caught up to her lips, gazing around. At the iced cake with Father Christmas standing on it like an explorer on an ice cap, a very big plinth for a very small statue. At the starry tree with the sweet pine scent warming out of it; at the doll's house. On that her eyes fix themselves. She goes up to Nora and whispers, 'Is that a dolly's house?' Living away in the country she has not seen one before, only heard of one.

'I think it must be.'

'Who is it for?'

Martin and Sylvia are brought in. Martin looks round as much as to say, 'What's all this about?' Sylvia grins: ('It's amusing, anyway').

'*Who* is it for, Mummy?'

The meal becomes a passion of suspense. 'Who is it for, the dolly's house?'

'Would it be for Sylvia?'

'Oh, no; she's not big enough.'

'Perhaps it's for Martin.'

'But boys don't have dolls.'

'Do you think it's for Anthea?'

Even the Christmas cake, even chocolate biscuits are eaten absent-mindedly. At last, at last the doll's house. Sylvia has a pig whose tail whirls round by clockwork. Martin has a humming top and a drum. The rest of the day is a tattoo. On the parchment of the drum are traces of some old legal deeds, beautifully penned. Tum – tum – tum. So much for the law.

Outside, as I fed and closed up the animals, there was a glow in the sky, and from several directions the booming of church bells. They sounded like the guns of peace. A cloud blossomed behind the apple trees.

There was a sense as though one had a tryst here, remembering the apple blossom in the cloud, and the peace of the bells meeting and mingling their circumference of sound over the whole land.

FIVE

New Year

ICANNOT HELP FEELING a bit free today as I gaze at the ten-year-old motor in the shed. Ever since one took that fatally easy step and learned to drive, long ago, one has never felt quite one's own master. I say easy: it was then. No driving tests. All you needed was five shillings for a licence. It was a van I bought: being a farmer it seemed to me the most useful. Sometimes we took livestock, sometimes people. Pigs, calves, sacks of meal, coal. The journey with the calves was exciting. There was nothing between the driving seat and the rest of the van but a thin rail for the driver to lean his back on. We lifted the calves in at the back and they immediately tried to jump out at the front. I drove: my brother sat beside me, facing back, and wrestled with those two calves for eight miles. The van was made of tin, a resounding vehicle. People we passed needed no horn to warn them of our approach: they skipped on to the bank and stared as we went by, wondering whatever was happening inside that van.

I learned to drive in the simplest possible way. The man who delivered the van took me up the road and down the road: that was my tuition. And once you can drive, somehow you are kept at it. It is, 'Oh, would you mind running so-and-so home?' A matter of twenty miles perhaps. Hours, days, slip away. Driving to me was never anything but an exhausting waste of time. I bless the increased tax, the increased price of petrol, the rationing of it – the whole combination that has definitely put the motor beyond the means of a poor man with three children.

But Nora – she did not drive, and she suffers from chilblains. She is equally of the view that motoring is quite out of the question now: she cycles cheerfully along with me to market. But on our way home she did not sing, as I did, at sight of Venus, the evening star, above the last red bar of sunset cloud. 'I won't mind it,' she said, 'not a bit, when it isn't quite so cold.' With that she busked first her right arm, then her left, swaying like a skater as the crammed rush baskets on the handlebars swung with the swaying arm.

I have a good bicycle. Its make? The Lidgate. Never heard of it? Perhaps not: and if one day you are passing through Lidgate and you look for a big factory turning out mass-produced cycles, you will not see it. No, but over a stream and up a bank there stands a shop with R.E. Jolley written up. He is the maker of 'The Lidgate' cycle. When I farmed near Lidgate, in course of a chat with him one day, I had a deal with him over one of his bicycles. It cost me four pounds ten, and I have had it twelve years, and I would not take four pounds ten for it today. A strong, easy-running machine; and every time I take it out I think of my good friend, Mr Jolley, and the talks we used to have, up there overlooking the pretty village. The last time I was in that neighbourhood I called on him, and he came hurrying down and shook me by the hand, and up we went through the shop and into the parlour to see his wife and have a cup of tea. He had a whole shop full then of his good bicycles. I hope he is still in business. If you want a good bicycle, get a Lidgate. You can carry such a lot on it. My old market bag, a little bolster-shaped thing, but of such leather as you would hardly see today, fits beautifully on to the carrier.

The only thing wrong with our local town, I find, is that the kerbs are skimpy. They will not support a bicycle properly. One tends to choose shops where there is a deep kerb.

And when we are thoroughly-loaded, so that the carrier has slight tail-wag, and the handlebars have rush-basket pendulums, the clock is striking four and the winter day flushing down into the streets. The water is turning to ice in the puddles and crackles under the tyres. Across the river creeps a frosty mist. A waft of perfume out of the cinema, and then suddenly one is up in the glassy country silence. The trees become silhouettes, the sky is all bruised light. There is no wind. Smoke creeps

out of a cottage chimney. Sheets are frozen stiff on the line. A farm
exhales its odour, that is its soul, and wraps us in an aura of old England.
It is a smell that even seems to have warmth, the air is so scaldingly cold.
Puddles in the empty yard glitter: the shapes of the buildings have a look
of permanent purpose.

Down a hill and up a hill. I am a little behind Nora, waiting to see if
she is going to get off. 'I got off because I thought I heard you get off.'
On again: the level mile to home. Then I saw the evening star come out,
Venus above black pine trees, and I sang.

Home. Firelight, warmth, tea. One is proud of the packages ranged on
the table, to have brought them home by one's own muscle. In one of
Nora's are eleven yards of flannel for new nightdresses for the children.

Dripping toast, tea in big cups, an incandescent fire in the stove,
shutters up, curtains drawn. How many eggs today? Leaning back,
thinking of that ride. Talking of the purchases but thinking of the ride:
the smell of the farm, the star, the red bar in the sky. Things that fortify
against whatever the loudspeaker may have to say.

The tin bath is being prepared in front of the fire. Toys litter the floor.
Anthea is combing Sylvia's hair. 'I'm making her a lot of curls, because
she is getting a big girl now.' Topsy the doll has been naughty and was
put in another room by herself. 'And then I went to the door again
and I whispered with my ears, and she'd stopped being naughty.' Sylvia
is banging the dog on the back with the brush: she pulls her ear. The
dog, who would bite my hand off for much less, lies on a patchwork
cushion and merely looks mournful. Martin, seeing all this, tries to use
his humming top as a brush on his own head.

Picture books have suddenly come into favour, and the toy piano.
Martin, in a red jersey, naked from the waist down, standing by the
table looking profoundly wise, beating notes out of the toy piano. Sylvia
looks at a picture of ducks on the floor. Martin knows there is one of
dogs over the page. He goes and tries to turn it over, as he is good at
barking like a dog. Sylvia cannot bark, but is very good at 'Quack', so

she wants ducks still. A tussle: the cardboard page vertical, one hand pushing one side, one the other. Growls and squeals of anger. No sooner does Martin get the dogs than, flap, it is ducks again. Finally both ducks and dogs are lost in an upheaval, and now it is cows. They are both good at saying moo, so they obliterate the picture with eager hands and moo like anything.

This morning, left together in their playpen, they stripped yards of paper off the wall. So we moved the cupboard up against the patch, and life goes on.

Anthea shows me the new soles to her shoes: to have shoes mended is almost as good as having new shoes. What a lot of shoes they need. What a lot of clothes: yards and yards of material. One begins to realise what a big inter-family traffic there is in children's clothes. They are passed on and on. I had a friend when I was thirteen. We often stayed at each other's homes; bicycled together, fished for minnows. I grew a little older and became romantic about her. Later, when I grew up, our ways parted. One day I left my farm to go to London for her wedding. I remember a very hot day, and her elder sister talking hats to a friend all through the service. My friend has had three children, and now I have three; and we never see each other, but parcels of clothes go to and fro. Little woolly coats, frocks with ribbons, these are the connecting links. And when Anthea, Martin, or Sylvia have outgrown them they go on to someone else.

By way of small recompense I sent her one of our cockerels, trussed and garnished with sprigs of fresh parsley which I dug a foot and more into the snow to find. She wrote cheerfully from their country refuge (though things are most uncertain for them): 'Meanwhile we exist – happily, I must own; and I'm sure it's good for us.' It is fortifying to hear from friends, isolated in winter frost, waiting for what is to happen, yet living strenuously forward at the same time, bringing up a family.

There is a woman in the next village with seven children. Today we did up a parcel of these clothes and left them at her house. Her husband is a fisherman: she is alone for months with the seven.

From there we went on: the sun was summer-bright, the road dusty; the light cold wind scalded our faces. We came to the farm we were seeking, to buy some more pullets.

Crash! A boy who has been walking along a frozen stream cracking the ice with an axe, has fallen and cracked a great deal more with his behind. He gets up dripping, and with one look of mortification at us, that we have seen, departs silently through the fence. The poultry farmer among his pens looks up, too, as though that were a summons. 'Do you want to see me?' We approach. 'It is all right,' I say to Nora, 'he will sell us some pullets: there is something about that rocking horse.' It prances full gallop across the garden. There is something about a house with a rocking horse in the garden in January, so vigorous-looking, that predisposes one towards the inhabitants.

But 'No,' he says, 'I'm afraid I haven't any to spare: you see, the pullets are all in lay now.'

I agreed that of course it is the wrong time, and naturally he does not want to sell laying birds. Then I ask, 'Can you get enough food for all your flock?'

'It is a trouble,' he admits. 'Can you?'

'Well, we don't keep many more than enough to supply ourselves. I could manage to feed a few more, though.'

I go on talking quietly about this and that, just to give him time to think. I can see him thinking it over. He says, 'I don't know that I might not let you have a few, in view of the food situation.'

We go the round of his pens. Long-necked, egg-weighted pullets; gallant, glistening, embattled cocks. So tame, too. 'If you'll just stand there, we'll drive this lot into their house.' There is just one pigeon-hole opening into the house from their run. To try and drive a dozen ordinary hens into that, well, you could try all day. But these walk in in a minute. Handling them: 'No, not her, she's got rather a pale eye. This one —' (looking at a number on her ring and consulting a chart) '— she's laid four eggs. This one – she's laid three.'

He puts black-and-yellow striped rings on our birds.' We shall know yours when you come for them by the tigerish rings.'

What a great deal there is in poultry to the expert.

Of the first batch of hens I ever had in my life, bought from the outgoing farmer, the best layer was a skinny-looking creature with a cross beak.

Nine years ago today Nora and I were going to be married. It is a clear and frosty dawn. 'Now,' Nora says, 'I was upsetting my early tea in the bed, a thing I've never done before or since, and thinking the lace I had chosen did not go very well on the frock.'

Now, I was waking rather depressed that London should look so dark and dreary even on a fellow's wedding day. As much as to say, 'I don't care a damn.'

Today we are landed in the biggest war ever, with three helpless infants. Farming against the weather is nothing to it.

I say as I roll out of bed, 'I'll see if I can borrow Mr Prosser's chicken crate. He made it specially to go on a bicycle.'

Ten-thirty. Now Nora had managed to find some more satisfactory lace, and was sewing it on her frock. Now I was being treated to gin before the ceremony.

Today I am trying to fix Mr Prosser's chicken crate on to my carrier in his barn. It seems an insoluble problem: it looks like an elephant on a postage stamp. Mr Prosser is out. I remember now he said he has some sort of expanding carrier. I wheel the thing homeward, nevertheless. I meet a farmer friend who takes the crate aboard his car. He says, 'I lost my old horse this morning. He was twenty-eight. He was bound up: his muscles were paralysed: he hadn't passed anything since Saturday.'

Twelve o'clock. Now we were being married.

Here we are standing in the yard in the wind, with string, wire, and pieces of wood, trying to scheme how to fix the crate on the carrier.

Two o'clock. Now we were finishing our wedding breakfast, and a gleam of sun came out and shone on us, which people said was a good omen.

Now the children have been fed and dressed, and are going out with Ada, then to her cottage to tea. We, too, are setting out, having received by telephone an offer of more easily managed crates from our poultry farmer. Between us, we think, we can carry these slung about us somehow, to get the birds home. We have also, tied on behind, a cat bag. It is a thing handed down: we have stored it for years; and as we never go journeys with cats it seemed pointless. But it comes in useful. It has two holes, one at either end. I remember, as a child, travelling in a train, and first the cat's paw appearing through the hole, and then its nose, and the talk it started among the passengers about cats. I still expect to see that paw appear.

Now we were leaning back in a closed car, being whisked to Charing Cross.

Now, red-nosed, we are pedalling uphill against the wind. Riding a road regularly you know where to get off: up a hill, you make it a tree or something. Always on this hill we think we shall get right up it this time. Always, at the tree, we know we shall not.

Farm work is at a standstill owing to the frost. A man comes out of his cottage into a trim small meadow and whistles two yearling cattle to him. The cattle stand and look at him, but do not go to him. He stands on the other side looking at them, hands plunged vertically in his corduroy pockets.

A young woman is pushing a load of firewood in a handcart. It is a heavy load. She has a child, all red muffler and hood. She perches him on the load, making it still heavier. He laughs down at her, pixie-like, and she, trying to shove the cart into motion again, laughs up at him. She is pretty and gay and strong: in this game of pushing the handcart along she is no older than her child. They belong to some happy time – of yesterday or tomorrow – embalmed in the sunlight.

The old roadman on his tricycle is ahead, cycling with antique deliberation: his knees come out stiffly sideways as they crank over. A rather ragged man passes hurriedly on a bicycle that wheezes. A girl goes by, on her afternoon off, cycling blithely, as though to some music she hears in the air. People cycle characteristically, even as they walk: the ploughman homeward pedals ploughmanlike.

We reach the farm. Crates like Christmas hampers accommodate the birds. The last one goes into the cat bag. One long tail feather pokes out, accusatory.

Four o'clock. Nine years ago we were sitting in the buffet car of a train having tea.

Here we are starting homeward with our hens; the great crate behind me trying to push me off the saddle, the cat bag lashed to Nora's handlebars with a dirty handkerchief I found in my overcoat pocket. All the string had been used up on the hampers. The one bird in the cat bag is more trouble than all the rest, because first it goes forrard, then slips aft, upsetting the balance.

We arrive. I open the lid of a hamper: there they are sitting like the blackbirds in the pie, eyeing me curiously but unafraid.

Five o'clock. Now we were in another well-upholstered car, gliding to our hotel among the twinkling lights of a southern town.

Now, with the new moon looking on and Venus near, and the pigs squealing for their supper and Selina mooing softly for hers, we are doing things with wire netting; trying to let the old birds into the house without letting the new ones out. There is a meeting on the threshold: some come out. With guile, Nora standing still as a post, being a netting stake, we coax them back. By the time I close the door on the last one Nora is almost frozen to the netting she holds and it is dark.

While Nora is putting the children to bed I quieten the pigs and settle to milking against the comforting warmth of Selina's flank. Then I make a fire of logs in my little room, put up the shutters, draw the curtains, put a bottle of our wine to warm on the hearth, and light two new candles in the oaken sticks, and draw up two chairs.

That done, I sit, and bless this miracle of silence in a world at war.

('Nine years – that's a long time ago, Anthea – before you were born.' 'I *wasn't* born: I was here always.')

Seven o'clock. We were sitting in a hotel together having a glass of sherry and discussing the furnishing of our farm-cottage, and whether to buy an oil-cooking stove or not.

Now Nora comes in and shuts the door. I fill the glasses. We sit before our fire and discuss – what sort of a cooking stove shall we get now, seeing that our first one has become too small for our growing family.

One thing leads to another. Because of buying those birds I am now sitting listening to a lecture on place names. My poultry farmer is a member of the Archaeological Society, and by the following day I seem to be on the way to becoming one. First to return his crates, then to buy some kippers for the family. The lecture is at three. I arrive at a few minutes to, and the hall has but a sprinkling of people. 'A thin house today,' says our chairman. But at three minutes past, just as the lecturer is about to begin, people pour in, until not only is every seat full, but additional chairs have to be fetched.

I remark on this to my neighbour. She replies, 'On the contrary, that is very punctual – for us.'

Upstairs there is a soldiers' club, which also sounds to be full. We are reminded that army boots are heavy boots. To the left of the speaker and just behind his blackboard is a curtained archway. The curtain is in a state of nervous movement: a face appears, and is withdrawn again. I am in the back row. The audience, winter-muffled, look from here like a cloakroom; lots of stuff lying heaped on chairs, attentive-looking stuff.

The lecturer begins by warning us against making too easy assumptions in hunting down the meanings of place names. Dunwich, for instance, was originally a Celtic word meaning deep water, not the 'drab enchantress' that crossword puzzle-makers would have us believe. I learn that there is a Place Name Society, and wonder what would get one black-balled from it. Probably suggesting that Bury St Edmunds was so named because St Edmund was buried there. Or to be caught perpetrating a rebus on Bungay on the Society's notepaper. I learn that it has been established beyond doubt that by no means all the river names of England are Celtic. We, as East Anglians, are commiserated with for the fact that we have no records earlier than Domesday Book. That, to the place-name hunter, is as yesterday. It makes our task all the harder.

The fascination of the place-name game is the sort of conjuring trick whereby one word is turned into something totally different. You remember those humorous drawings which once had a vogue, whereby a slow old man for instance, was gradually transformed into a tortoise? The process in words is as subtle. Yet it looks easy. You explain that y = g, and substitute one for the other: that y was sometimes pronounced like e. That h before a consonant drops out; that f is elided. It seems you or I could do it? But that is just where we make a mistake. There are secret laws governing this jugglery, only learned perhaps after ordeal on being admitted to the Place Name Society.

Thus, in a minute our favourite village is proved to be no more than a tree stump. We stir restively. But look, it is so. The v becomes f, the e drops out; so Stoven ('the little saint gets to a hot place') deteriorates into Stofn, which is early Scandinavian for a tree stump. So that's your pretty village. If it had been even a tree – there is a pleasant pub called The Cherry Tree where I have had sociable drinks in summer. But a stump.

Copdock, now, that is a tree. He pulls the word to pieces: it comes apart like a well-made gadget, once you know how. Copped ac, i.e. copped oc, i.e. copped oak, i.e. a pollard.

'Yes,' I reply to my neighbour's whispered query, 'copped oak.'

'No,' she whispers back, 'I said, can you smell kippers?'

Kippers? What an idea. I sniff and sniff. Why, yes, there is a smell of kippers. Quite strong. Oh Lord, in my pocket where I thrust them when I bought them, in a hurry not to be late for the lecture. Three pairs of them, wrapped insecurely in 'Premier Denounces Germany'. I put in my hand and am met by an oily ooze. Essence of kipper is seeping through my coat. I lay my hat over the patch. 'Now you mention it I *can* smell kipper.'

A soldier enters precipitately from the street. He is cut off from his club by the learned phalanx of the Archaeological Society. The curtain of the arch becomes violently agitated: a hand emerges from it, with a crooked finger, beckoning. The soldier hesitates: he dare not make the crossing, and retreats to the street.

Four o'clock strikes. The lecturer looks at his wrist watch, an unconscious reflection on provincial time. 'I have been talking too long already, but I must give you one or two further examples.' He cleans the blackboard and starts again.

The talk becomes more fascinating the later it grows. There is a pretty fairy tale of a village whose name means 'The place of the dwarfs'. No one knew why. The only thing unusual about the place was a peculiar echo. Then somebody pointed out that the Celts had a belief that echoes were carried by 'the little people'. Hence the place of the dwarfs. Another name, meaning 'decorated floor', was incomprehensible till a Roman tessellated pavement was unearthed there.

It is a quarter past four. The curtain stirs again. This time a whole arm comes through, and suddenly we are in a flood of electric light. Several people are torn between the fascination of the subject and fear of the blackout, and get up, only to sit down again.

'I really have gone over my time,' admits the speaker, 'but in conclusion I should just like to mention this.' The blackboard is wiped blank again. This time the teaser is Hoxne, pronounced, as we all know, Hoxen. That looks an easy one; but no, it has baffled generations of experts. From Hoxne to Hoxana: that takes us back a thousand years, and we still are not far from Hoxne. However, a sage at last solved it. Let x stand for cks, he said. Then cks can stand for chs. Now do you see where we are getting? Why, to hock-shin; in other words, a horse's shinbone. Still in the dark? A piece of land shaped like a horse's shinbone, from which the place took its name. Cf. Nesbit = nose-bit.

What would happen if I dared, but I daren't, get up and suggest that Hoxne, pronounced Hoxen, equals just oxen?

Obviously those Viking settlers set that booby trap for just such a future mug as me.

Four-thirty. Yet the best is still to come. If Copdock equals copped oak, then what is Baldock but bald oak?

So people thought for a long time, until somebody discovered that in the fourteenth century the Knights Templars held the manor of Baldock. They were crusaders: they had been to the East, to Baghdad, which was then called Beldag. They named Baldock after Baghdad. So the very English town of Baldock on the edge of the Cambridgeshire cornland plain is nothing more or less than Baghdad.

With this the meeting closes amid applause – and an odour of kippers.

SIX

The cold strengthens

SNOW YESTERDAY, snow last night, snow this morning. Everything is covered. It is still snowing. I shovel away at the snow to clear a path, while still it snows. There is something futile about shovelling snow; it is in great bulk, yet it is light as nothing. It is like trying to throw a feather. It laughs at you. So I shovel, shovel at nothingness, like shovelling in a dream.

When it is snowing or raining, so that the children cannot go out, then it is a custom that there shall be music in the parlour. The parlour to us is half what it is, and half a memory of itself under another roof, with another view. But to the children it will be always what it is. Far away into the year 2000 will go a memory of the tub-back chair standing in the corner, with the picture of the old woman darning on the wall above. And the writing table with brass rings instead of drawer knobs beside the window that looks out upon the crab apple tree. And Nora's work table with the flowers painted on it and the little drawers that run in and out as smooth as silk, and the lids and compartments.

These things, to Anthea, Martin and Sylvia, will stand in their places as from everlasting to everlasting. The room will be spoken of, and their combined memories will illumine the more shadowy corners. Starting from now, from the exciting thing the room now is; the treat for a wet day or a snowy one.

The snow gives me a holiday, too. And a holiday, when you grow older, consists in allowing yourself to take a long time doing a thing which you usually do, if at all, in a hurry.

So I get my land boots out, and wash them and saddle-soap them. How indissoluble Suffolk mud can be, adhering in hard little knobs in creases and corners, melting slower than trodden snow. Under winter's mud is autumn's mud of the sugar beet field. And what a difficult thing a land boot is really to get a grip of. Then when they are dry, I get out the dubbin and smear them all over, and rub it in, using the mud scraper that Grandfather has shaped like a wooden knife to press it in all along where the upper meets the sole. How my mother would have loved to see me doing this, to whom it was far more excellent that I should dubbin my boots than write a book.

Their suppleness is something good to feel after all this. Now they sit, black and shining, almost a bit smug-looking. It seems a shame to make them dirty themselves again.

Now the music has started. In the parlour Anthea is sitting beside Nora at the piano, with a book of nursery rhymes in front of them. They are playing 'Boys And Girls Come Out To Play'. Anthea watches how Nora does it, and dings away at her end of the scale, chanting at the same time in a high, declamatory voice. It is interesting to watch her singing: she goes blank-looking, as they say old folk singers do, completely rapt, immersed in her song. And though the feminine members of the household insist that she has a very good idea of the tune, to me it is less of a tune than a declamation, with a curious little half-tone drop at the end of a line. At the same time the ding-ding-ding of the flat of her hand on three notes marks the rhythm inexorably.

While Nora is reading the music Anthea is reading the picture of boys and girls with hoops and dogs that run round the page.

> Come with a whoop, come with a call,
> Come with goodwill or ne'er come at all.

'That,' says Anthea, pointing to a figure of a terrier chasing after them, 'is Ne'er.'

Ritual is inborn: ritual and a sense of property are as complete in a child as its fingers and toes. What has happened before must happen again, to the last detail. Nora starting to play and sing another song is stopped. 'No, I sing this one all by myself.' It is 'Goosey Goosey

Gander'. Next comes 'Curlylocks'. For some reason this is very affecting; whether on account of the words, the contrast between feeding the swine and sitting on a cushion eating strawberries and cream, or the lilt of the tune, or both, we cannot tell. Anyhow, Nora hurries through it, making almost swing music of it to jolly it up. All the same, before the end of it, Anthea has lost her voice and her eyes blink swiftly. Finished, Nora would turn the page, but Anthea whispers, 'Again.'

The next song is stopped as soon as it is started. Anthea is wriggling protestingly. 'Why, of course,' Nora says, 'I forgot,' and lifts her down off her two cushions. She starts again. 'This is the way we wash the clothes.' Anthea down on the floor does a slow and solemn pantomime. Washing, sweeping, baking, going to church. Then she climbs back upon her chair and is ready for the next song. If in the singing of the many verses of any one of them Nora makes a mistake of one word, Anthea corrects her loudly, and the line has to be sung again.

Now Grandma comes in with the twins. Martin struts about, staring at the still strange room, and finally posts himself by Anthea at the piano, staring alternately at the notes going up and down, and the mouths opening and shutting. Sylvia in Grandma's arms gives it all a cursory glance, and interests herself in the quality of Grandma's clothes. Martin, whose eyes are on a level with the keyboard, stares for a long time, then slowly reaches up a hand, gripping the piano with the other, and knocks a note. From now on it becomes a trio. Till Anthea gets into a reverie, staring back at Sylvia, and the song dies on her lips. Martin has seen the big mirror. Nora is left playing nursery rhymes to herself.

Mirror supersedes music. Martin is stood up in front of it. He looks first at us, then at us in the mirror. They are here, yet they are there: what is the solution? His eyes get wider and blacker. Sylvia is held up to it. She quickly takes it for granted that there should be two of everybody. Anyhow, she is not going to worry about it. Grandma swings her to her reflection: she laughs uproariously.

Martin is not amused. To be waved at in the mirror makes it the more puzzling. He struts round the room very worried-looking.

Anthea is still eating tea. The tray has gone, the table is cleared, all but for Anthea's plate with a large piece of chocolate cake on it, and a bun at the side. She waves goodbye to the others returning to the parlour. It is not that she eats so very much, but she stops for minutes at a time, lost in meditation. Watching her and her four-year-old rotundity I think, well, things do solve themselves. Remembering how worried Nora used to be about her tiny appetite, trying to tempt her with this and that. There she sits munching her way through the cake, and looking at it approvingly and rocking her head from side to side, as she always does

when she is enjoying something. As the left hand puts the last piece of cake in her mouth, the right hand is closing over the bun; 'Because it was such a small piece of chocolate cake.'

As this nears its end, 'Now you can go, Father, because I can open the door myself, you know.' She has just learned to do this, so I take myself off. Soon a shout, and Anthea with her plate has nearly reached the bottom of the stairs. She is triumphant, and runs along the passage shouting, 'I opened the door myself and came downstairs with my hand full of plate.'

The parlour furniture, pushed to the sides of the room, leaves an expanse of carpet. Here on a cushion Sylvia contorts herself till she rolls off. She laughs and climbs on again. Martin struts like a comedian continually journeying towards something against which to fall. Instead, he stops midway, half sits down, half falls forward, steadies himself, and starts again.

Anthea finds something: 'What is this?'

'A mushroom.'

'A mushroom, Mummy? What for?'

'It's for mending stockings, dear: you put it under the hole, so.'

'What did you say?' (Meaning, 'I don't understand.')

'Let me show you.'

Martin gets it and runs off with it: then Sylvia bags it and carefully puts it behind her. This she does with every toy, till she has a pile. Martin, though twice as big, gets worsted always, because he is not so persistent. He starts something else. The best thing in the parlour to him is the doorknob. Because it is the secret of escape. Already he wants something else: he wants the rest of the house. The doorknob is a talisman. If Father or Mummy shake it the door opens: but if I shake it the door doesn't open. One day when I shake it the door *will* open. Meantime go on shaking.

There are two opposite efforts – the dog's to get into the room, and Martin's to get out. They await, on either side of the door, their chance. It comes with my entry. The dog with a growl ('Stop me if you dare') and a fury of feet, gets in: Martin collides with me. I stand him up. 'Well – now what?' With freedom before him he pauses uncertainly. He cocks his head, alert, curiously resistant on his stout shoulders, held in a sort of gyroscopic balance. There he stands, and the passage goes off into darkness. The stairs are lit; but he knows the stairs. So thrusting his right leg forward, which brings his shoulder swinging round like a boxer's, he sets off towards the darkness.

Anthea is delighted. She dances after him, shouting in a mock grown-up way, 'Now Martin, where *do* you think you're goin' to?' Martin takes no notice. He is utterly alone, with a puzzled, defensive tilt of the head, strutting on. He comes to a twilit threshold: beyond it is quite dark. He pauses there; then he gets down on his knees and crawls forward. The light is turned on. He finds himself face to face with himself in a mirror. The old problem.

He is carried back protesting into the warm, into the parlour. A bout of ring-o'-roses as a diversion. Anthea likes the going round part, the twins the falling down part. So it all ends in a heap. Martin pulls himself out of it and makes straight for the doorknob again.

Enter David Caponeth with his wife in a snowstorm. And exit again after a drink, beating for home against the gale. His little car neat and bright stood outside the door, luffed into the wind. And he squeezed himself in as of old. It used to be a very little car, and he filled it like a tight suit of clothes. Little cars have got a little larger, but so has David, his beard, his hat, his coat. All his life he has been a sailor – a sailor of small boats on big oceans, and now he has retired to a little house in an Essex byway and is in heaven. Occasionally he writes a sea story and sells it about six times over. I can never sell a thing more than once and am happy to do that, but David has a sort of 'ahoy there' acquaintance with all the world, and his stories appear both here and in earnest little American towns who pay well for a bit of culture.

The thing about his Essex cottage is – it is still his ship. Everything is shipshape. His dining room is like a cabin – I don't mean consciously.

He has had enough of the sea. Being a real sailor he is now interested in the land. But he has been so used to confined quarters that he does not know how to expand. He makes such a clean, clear boundary of his place; digs out a ditch and heaps the earth into a bulwark against his hedge. Neat hedge, neat garden. And he paces about, casting a weather-eye aloft, from boundary to boundary in about half a dozen strides.

Sitting having breakfast in his room, though you are set fast in Essex clay, you are still sailing the world. He is drinking very strong coffee in a mug, reading a letter from Cyprus. Vaguely Scandinavian, bare-wood utensils stand about. The bread is so English, so coarsely wheaten, as now has come to look foreign.

His car, too, has a sort of nicety about it, swabbed clean like the hull of a ship.

When he and his wife came to see us they were staying near, and were going to be with us for the day. But the increasing snow decided them to run for home. Even so it was something to see them even for twenty minutes. David is a big man in a small way; a small way for choice. He is prosperous in a small way – his way. He is not going to puff and pant after 'success'. With him you feel that America is only a stone's throw away, the East next door. He wears the world, he makes it come to him, it floats around his cottage in Essex.

And always something heartening. Last time it was something very good about the power, speed and precision of our mechanised troops. While the papers blare about unreadiness, the real people, the men of steel, are just waiting the moment to strike, quiet and ready.

This time it was, 'Do you know that 43 per cent of the present German recruits are rejected unfit? The outcome of guns instead of butter. The whole thing is rotten, ready to collapse.'

His bearded emphasis holds me spellbound. Has one's wishful thinking been all the while well-founded?

Well, now they have gone homeward in the snowstorm, David and his wife, and left me to these hopeful speculations.

A pity that they grow grey and doubtful as the echoes of that reverberate and resourceful figure fade, and one is left with just the snow falling as before.

One thing there was no doubt about, and that was the bushel of apples David left for us in a sack. They are spice apples and come off the two great trees that stand in the middle of, that are the very mast and rigging of, his shipshape garden. These apples invite no one to steal them, they are green and rough and sour-looking; but the taste – that is superb. I have plenty of apples in my orchard, but I have not these apples – could not grow them; they are local to his Essex clay. It is not too much to say that the life of that great nomad, David, is camped around those trees. He clambers up and down them, checking American blight, cutting out dead wood. They overspread his ground, but lesser fruits must take their chance; these take a man's lifetime to come to full fruition.

So I lay his gift of apples carefully among my own. While there are apples in the box autumn reaches on through winter. Under the straw in the shed mine are rosy as though newly kindled by the light I let in.

> Where, alack,
> shall Time's best jewel from Time's chest lie hid?

Why, here in this old grocer's box under straw and a sack. In the autumn with all the gold and red and yellow of leaves and flowers I never knew them, busily picking, hastening because of the coming shower. But now, with the eternal snow all round, their colour is wonderful, gladdening. I had forgotten that earth could do such things.

The well-known odour, as when I lifted the lid years back on my school box, where books and apples were all packed together. Half the term my Latin grammar smelt of apples. But all one cared about an apple then was to get one's teeth into it. Later a man needs other comforts. To look at the colour, the sunlight-suffusion freaked with that chippy red on one side. How did it happen? How could frozen Nature have ever nourished such a smile?

It is better than taking a warm egg out of the nest, to go with snow on one's boots and get a basketful of these keeping apples.

Picking them was living in a different world for a day or two. A tree-top world. Thence looking down into the tree was like being caught by an enormous spider. The trunk was but a nexus of writhing boughs, whose twigs caught me as I forced upward to the top of the ladder. One grabbed me under the collar, another tried to pick my pocket, a third would have lifted me off the ladder by the seat of my trousers and dangled me like a ripe apple. As for my hat, that had been snatched by several boughs in competition, and left far below.

Having forced myself up to the top I attained a sort of apple life. There is something rare about being close up to the apple in its height, almost cheek to cheek as it hangs, sharing its solitude. While the apple hangs there, it is inviolate; however near you come, it is perfectly to itself, its life the life of the wind.

As I take an apple from the dish now, with the snow-laden gale from the sea rattling the shutters, I wonder if it is one of those I picked from the top of the tree, in view of many fields, of the harvests of a dozen farms, and the summer sun focused to a point of light in its shiny skin, making a little cosmos of it.

Or one picked at that moment when Martin, after trying to trace my voice, was so surprised to see Father appearing out of the top of a tree that he upset his pram and lay howling, while I made a speedy and yet seemingly slow descent.

It is February, and we have plenty of apples yet. Yesterday I looked them over and found no more than half a dozen bad. And this in the hardest winter for forty years. I do not wrap each up or lay them in trays. Just pack them into a grocer's box and cover it with straw and a sack or two. There they lie in the shed and colour themselves red and gold, that were green when laid in. Till they have the tones that are in wine and firelight and old masters.

* * *

There is something staring, insane, about the snow. Every man looks homeless in it. A black, lean, puppyish retriever goes gambolling about, plunging in and out of drifts, anybody's and everybody's dog. He follows a grey lean-nosed woman up the road: won't be shooed away. At last, exasperated, she turns and runs at him. After trudging with difficulty so far, she runs back, flapping her arms to shoo the dog. She only loses the ground she has gained. The dog thinks it a great game. She plods on again. By the time the local bus comes in sight he has grown tired of her, though, and attached himself to me. He swaggers out in front of the bus, and it pulls up with a hoot and a jerk. The driver wears a helmet like a flying man.

The bus doubles on its tracks, taking in every possible village on its way to the town. For a shilling return you see the country. You get within a mile and a half of the town – in sight of it – then roundabout for another four miles, coming in from another quarter.

People complain about this, but I say what's the hurry? It is a good shillingsworth.

We pick up the woman who tried to chase off the dog. The door opens in a patient way. It lets in a freezing draught, so it is opened and closed every time someone gets in. 'No, not that handle: the middle one – now push.' There is a boy of about twelve in the front seat, who luckily soon gets the hang of this from the driver. 'Open the door, sonny – shut the door, sonny.'

The woman with the lean Wellington nose looks out, prodding the window with it as the bus jolts, and blinking her deep-sunken eyes. What is she looking for, looking at the landscape as though it were a needle case? Or is it just a habit?

Others get in, recognise friends, ask after each other's health, and chat. Sitting together, bouncing in unison on the same seat and chatting, with their country hats and parcelled up in their country coats. While the airman-driver charges full speed at a snowdrift in a hollow; and the bus dashes in, groans and grinds and lurches, and drags itself out on the other side like a wounded animal. The village women bounce a bit higher but do not pause in their chat.

In front of me, alone and silent, sits a woman with the blackest of hair and a black Robin Hood sort of hat on it. She half turns her head, looking out of the window. There is something unusual about her profile: unusual here, that is. The high cheekbones, the full curves of her cheek and nostril and chin. There is something generous about the curves of her face. They are like variations of the same curve, and that a sort of question mark. Even her ears are different, apple-round, though nipped and spoiled by blobs of earrings. And her mouth has a quiet, internal smile as she looks out over the snow-covered landscape. She looks at it differently from the others: the grey woman worrying at it with her beaky nose, the gossips flicking glances at this or that house and going off into personalities. But she stares at the whole of it, as though writing her thoughts on those calm fields of snow. Her coat is black: smart and flimsy, with a collarless, square-shouldered wrong sort of smartness for her head and neck. Not like the coats of the country women, with blobs of different-coloured wool stuck on them, big and bag-like. Odd how tragic the collarless line of that coat makes her quiet contained grace of head and neck: it gives a hard, cut-price look to the generous curves of her flesh. She is, I realise, a refugee from Central Europe, several of whom are in houses about here. Perhaps she comes from Vienna or from Prague, detached into the English snow.

Yet the snow seems to denationalise the country, too. Black and white, a conglomeration of poultry sheds shine – red and white the houses. Such contrasts are not at home here. We pass a young wood with black slivers of trees, and someone dragging a sledge up a hill. Snow silver-glimmering between the slivers of the trees.

A great red bus with steamed windows meets us – hot-looking; and we, who are only a washed-out blue, have to back. We pass a roadman, with spade shouldered, handsome – as though the crisis of the snow had knit his brow with power. The shapes of it drifted against the hedges are wild. Great sagging lips of it, a generosity of contour, a fantasy of shape, so that our gentle-natured England is drowned, and the elemental forces have overwritten all, scrawled strange and foreign smiles upon the land. The skies have come down on us, and the old signs of our local life look perished and ineffectual; bits of wire netting on stakes, fruit trees turned to faggots – a whole fruit farm become a few last hairs on the universal baldness.

About every mile or so some lonely figure is standing at a corner. An old man gets in with a dangerous-looking stick; one of those old men of whom you are not sure whether they need helping or not; he looks at you as though he is looking at the distance.

'They never brought the snowplough down my road till this morning,' he says, standing up gripping the seat in front of him. He continues to stand, as though wanting to address the whole bus. But it starts with a jolt and he is jerked into a seat.

In the snow it looks as though the old life will never resume. Does our village England sleep under that sheet – the green sward and the sleek thatch? Will the pond ruffle again and sparkle with ducks? There is something gaunt and death-like in the angular shapes of houses under the pall. A garden swing hangs stiff with its load of snow.

The snow and the war are made one now; our life is buried. And the local bus carries us through country that is no longer our country; where a roadman stands who is no longer a roadman, but carries his shovel like a weapon. And the profile of the woman looking out in homeless thought, smiling past pleasure and past pain, alive with another sort of life than has ever yet made its home here.

While a placid, wrinkled village woman, robust, with short grey hair, sits dinging undaunted on the old home topics. She is like the last apple at the bottom of the box, old but sound, firm with the sweetness of summer.

I am right about the Robin-Hood-hat woman. As she gets out she pays, saying, 'One shilling, mistake.' The correct phrase is 'a shilling return'. When the bus started to run the proprietor said he would do it as cheaply as the train. The fare used to be one and twopence. Then the railway reduced theirs to a shilling. So the villagers refused to pay more than a shilling in the bus. Hence the phrase 'a shilling return'.

I have just time to get to the dentist. People who look cold make me feel colder. The soldiers look the coldest of all. The whole conversation of the little town is sniff-sniff. The dentist's assistant is amazingly cheerful, as though life were the greatest joke in the world. I sit, studying the dentist's ceiling. How well I know the ceilings of dentists, what they are made of, the mouldings, cracks, shadows, the old fly that hangs by a thread. And that peculiarly drab angle of the building opposite and the pattern of electric wires. And the particularly drab sort of birds that flit across the window, dusty sparrows. But here there are not sparrows but seagulls. Every now and then in the dead sky a great whitish-grey bird appears and disappears. While the dentist pokes and scrapes and prepares his drill. I thought, it won't be much, just a stopping come out. One forgets for months together about one's teeth, that being a civilised man the good times are but an interval and that one day again the crash will come. Often one leaves it till one gets used to the hole, it becomes part of the pattern of one's mouth, and when at length you go to the dentist, he prods and says, 'Hm, yes. I'm afraid —'

But for once I have been virtuous and gone early. Even so down comes the drill, till there seems hardly any tooth left. Grinding away on the edge of pain. And staring at the ceiling – a pale green ceiling – I reflect.

Strangely quiet, the little town: very few cars, only silent bicycles and people walking. Footsteps are silent in the snow, you only hear the sniff-sniff as they pass. The silence and the snow, yet many people: it is almost uncanny; a sort of numb mingling, dream-death-like; and a touch of the medieval in the hoods that all the women and children wear. And men wearing knitted helmets like Norman chain mail.

But it is almost more than a similitude; I feel it in the quiet air that projects the spirits of the old, old houses: they, too, are hooded, their sharp dormers peaked with snow. There is a new deathly cold possession of the past; and I feel as though we were fated to return through a darkness of time, to a world familiar to our forefathers.

The war is more than bombs, it is a state of being. I feel it in the furtive quiet of the town. It is the soul of civilisation that has fallen, caved in, long-decayed, hollow: and everybody goes furtively, knowing that the end has come.

About half past four I am aware of something about the town that is odd. And then I realise that what is odd is that it looks ordinary. It is dusk but not yet blackout time, and all the shops are lit up and shining into the street. In the market square my blue bus awaits dim and ghostly. In its darkness there is a stirring as if poultry have gone to roost, which tells me it is nearly full. The bulk of the driver can be seen standing up inside the front of the bus facing the assembled passengers. He stands there like Charon waiting for the shades. Really it is as though the little town were the frontier-post of death. And here we are – our pitcher broken at the fountain – fated for the journey.

'The thing is – you lose so much power: it's a job to get through,' our Charon is saying. 'She's got no power at all in the snow.'

There is a silence and you can hear the chewing of sweets, a comfortable masticating. A complex confectionery odour pervades the bus. I wish that I, too, had bought a bag of sweets.

'Is Mrs Lovey here?' the driver asks. She makes her presence known. 'Anybody else?'

Everybody is here except one who has got a lift with a friend, the driver is informed.

'That's a good job – I don't want to have to stop at the bottom of that hill.'

Suddenly there is a sort of scuffle at the door. It is the foreign lady: she is laden with parcels, some of which fall. The driver carries them down the bus for her. She sits behind me this time, in a nest of parcels.

I have learned, between masticating intervals, that she is keeping house for a Suffolk farmer.

The complicated door is shut. The driver swings into his seat. While we have been sitting here the town has quenched itself: the darkness is complete, we are all dead.

A couple of tiny lights are switched on in the bus, and we come to have a ghostly sense of one another.

There are more people than there were coming in. Two elderly countrymen, one with a sack over his arm, sitting side by side, erect as though in the hard, straight-backed chairs they have been accustomed to. There is something reassuring about these men: they might be angels, they are so glowingly of the country to which we are going. They are so at home in it that their very phrases have a prepared, pre-ordained cadence. The smile on the face of the one nearest me is not a smile of amusement but of disposition. His birdlike glances at me are curious and welcoming. Such, I feel, will know how to cope with the life to come. They can pick up the thread of their ancestry.

Outside the town it is lighter. There are golden clouds to the west, a substantial sunset. We bump and lurch more than ever, but the thing is in Charon's hands, and I let myself go with it, and watch the snowdrifts foaming past in contours that rise and fall. The two labourers sit rigid and smiling; the refugee and I relaxed, at a loss, filled with the cold wonder of the world. A cloud-world, one of the transitional circuits of the heavens, and our blue bus swinging through space.

We meet a lorry: it sidles gingerly, and we sidle round it. Then we stop and the driver goes back to see if they want towing out into the fairway again. They are all right, they say, and we leave them, digging at the back wheels, scattering the snow like dogs.

Lonely tracks lead away into the dusk. Here and there one or two get out and go plodding over the waste.

In the most desolate spot the two labourers get out. There is no home or hut in sight. But they know where they are going.

We pass houses in a hollow: they are all black-shut and enigmatic. A church, and opposite a glebe with oak trees standing in it like people.

The bus twists and turns; it is night outside, dark but ghostly with snow. I have no idea where we are. The human chatter in the bus by contrast with the snow-leagues crackles like a good fire.

But the extraordinary thing would be, if one could see not the people but their thoughts, lonely or intervolved, roaming. The woman in front of me kissing the hooded bundle in her arms, the pale blob of a face. So careful as she gets out and stumbles, shopping bag and baby, towards a deserted-looking cottage. And the refugee behind me, her thoughts, inaccessible, but rubbing against the small-windowed, clean-kitchen minds of the cheerful villagers chattering and laughing.

We stop at another empty-looking cottage and the driver hoots. Nothing happens. We set a woman down here in the afternoon. 'Yes, she said she was going to wait to ride home,' one of the passengers says. So Charon hoots again. In a minute a door opens. 'Here she comes. Come on, Liza, we almost gave you up.' Liza bustles in and becomes part of the conversation.

All this time I have been in a slack, suspended state of mind. Slack to the quivering and plunging of the bus, lost to the road.

But now I begin to have a vague notion of time and place. I get up towards the front of the bus. The driver knows exactly where each of us is to get out and stops there. 'Yours is the white gate on the right,' he says.

A white gate – how long ago? The bus has become home. But I am dropped out into the darkness. A white gate. Yes, here it is. It leads me along a path that is like a thread of memory, to a door, and suddenly a brightly-lit, warm interior – a life. Wife, children, relatives, and my own room, empty, waiting, with firelight on the walls.

I am turning a dunghill, black and steaming in the glittering snow. The air is the coldest yet: long icicles make ordinary little bushes fantastic. Turning dunghills and ditching – that was the winter work of Suffolk fishermen home from the aurora borealis, in the days when farmers in this parish grew twenty coombs an acre. Land and sea husbandry being thus intimately connected.

Feeding, littering, thawing drinking troughs – there is plenty to do. And making a bonfire round the pump, to thaw that. This morning our first conversation was about frozen pipes. We roamed imaginatively through the attic, considering which was frozen and where. I got out of bed in a tangle of pipes. But a slow black rook roaming across the sky of the window put my mind into a lazy, flapping motion – who cares? Who cares? There is a copper in the scullery and a soft-water well, whose pump looks as though it were one of the first products of the Iron Age, like the primitive steam engine, and has a little embossed design just above where, if it were a person (and sometimes it looks like a person), its navel would be. Its handle is old and hammered-out-looking, and so loose it is like shaking a tired man by the hand.

I hear Anthea coming downstairs, right foot first every time, then she runs along the hall and calls at the kitchen door, 'Please, may I come in? Is there anybody there?'

I like the way she sings it out, like a nursery rhyme. There is so much of crisis about life this morning. Cans of hot water being rushed upstairs, the copper fire being dived at to see if it has gone out, fuel being carted. So it is good to see a rook with his back turned on us all, napping slowly across the frozen blue, and to hear Anthea's singing voice. All the slack of life is taken up this frozen day; except for that song in the voice, 'Please can I come in?'

After dinner Anthea, wrapped and rosy, goes out into the snow. It sparkles in the sun: fifty yards away there are infinitesimal facets that flash. The intensity of their sparkle travels far to the eye. Anthea has been promised a snowman. But Nora temporises by drawing pictures in the snow with a stick. She calls me from my dunghill. At first I pretend not to hear. Somehow the pleasure of handling snow has gone from us. Anthea builds a castle of snow with her wooden spade. The snow so deep and white is rather solemn to be among. When it comes to the snowman we shamelessly make the 'castle' do for his body. We have only a head to make. The snow is so dry it won't compress. Only a very little head results from two pairs of very cold hands. Some withered bits that were flower clusters are stuck in the top. 'That's his hair.' But it does not look at all like hair, nor very much like a man. More like a white Christmas pudding with a bit of dead holly on top. Anthea looks at the object. 'When shall we do something else?'

So Nora takes her for a run down the road where the snowplough has been. What remains is smooth and hard and squeaks under the feet. How tender the tree trunks look, sun-haunted: the deep light is like a substance on them. Theirs is the only colour in the world, and the startled-looking red house.

Anthea stops suddenly and looks half distressful, half smiling, as she lifts and presses one foot against another. 'What is it – are your feet cold?' She does not say. It is that her feet are tingling after standing knee-deep in gumboots so long, and she does not understand the feeling. So they run again. Again she stops and looks puzzled. They run and run, and suddenly she becomes cheerful and talkative again, and glows and kicks up the snow.

Again the water troughs are frozen. But across the sky, like missives from the sun, go light golden clouds. Leaving everything I get round behind the stable and stare at the low sun and that high summery sky. I would live in that sky for five minutes. Somehow it is Italy, it is the background of an old master. Then, against the black conifer there, it is Scandinavia, the clear blue north. As I stare, noting the whispy, changing, ever-parting shapes, ghosts of shapes, it is summer England, and the lilac white with blossom, not with snow.

Odd at this stage to be affected by Akhnaton's daughter. But her statue reproduced in a book on past civilisations has made something special of this evening. Before my fire, surrounded by snow and fog, the stillness of a dead world, like a pause in time, I have read this book, showing that there is no such thing as progress – no slow dawning – but only rents in darkness. Massacre and torture – and then suddenly the flowering of an exquisite sensibility, as in this statue – a vital control. Today, we are farther from achieving what the sculptor of 3000 BC achieved than perhaps ever before. That is literal truth. Ours is the age of mechanical perfection and therefore of perfect loss of sensibility. For the perfect surface is the surface without sensibility. The springs are dry, while the opportunity is illimitable. If to our modern range of mental experience could be brought, intact, the dynamism of the savage —

But to be near to the sense of that much deeper power than the modern scene could ever have given one a hint of, which has run within man since he stood upright – that is a new warmth to the heart in these days, making these days small and short – even though the promised land be outside one's personal vision.

That is faith, even if there is no personal resurrection in it. Perhaps a birth of faith.

At this moment I hear Anthea come running downstairs. 'I want a piece of canvas,' she shouts in vibrant, triumphant excitement to which the word canvas seems strangely irrelevant. Until I remember that yesterday for the first time she really made something. By stitching various coloured wools through a square of canvas and then (with help) sewing it on to a piece of cloth, she made a kettle holder. Now she wants to make another.

The excitement – did I say the springs were dry?

It was lovely when the mildness came again yesterday, and I started pruning. Standing happily breathing the dank and misty air, and enjoying again the sight of myriad beads of dew instead of icicles.

After tea I had Martin on my knee at the piano, and Nora had Anthea on hers, so there were six hands at work on it. Then Sylvia came along and spread hers out most professionally on the keys. But finding the notes were not detachable, she became interested in the reflections on the polished surface of the back.

We sang some old English songs; then one about the spring:

> The Spring is coming, resolved to banish
> The King of the Ice with his turbulent train.
> With her fairy wand she bids them all vanish,
> And welcomes the sunshine to earth again.

'That one again,' Anthea said. And when they had gone up to bed, as she had her bath, 'Sing that song about the spring again, Mummy.'

SEVEN

The earth crumbles

A FTER THREE DAYS in bed, three days and three nights of illness, I am sitting at the window of my room, listening to the birds and feeling the sun. While I lay abed the snow went and the birds began to sing, and down there in the earth under the window are crowds of snowdrops that take the wind all together. After three days of brain-ache I cannot read, I cannot think; only sit and be thankful for the sun. Such small things as snowdrops moving in the wind become eventful; the way each is hung upon the curved stem, and their whiteness against the black earth, so quick after the dead white of the snow.

I am grateful that the wind is in the north, so that, though it moves the trees, the air is calm at this open south window, and sun-warmed. I stretch out my hand; the bricks of the house are warm and have attracted one or two flies. I can see quite a long way from this upper window. The white horse is harrowing the ten-acre field. Ten acres of earth crumbled level, and the blue-black woods beyond, and the white horse treading to and fro all day with slow elastic movement, white as the snowdrops are against the earth.

To my thankful eyes there is no monotony in that going to and fro, but a beauty that grows by continuance. A woman in a red tam-o'-shanter comes with the man's dinner basket: her disruptive note of red, bobbing into the field, interrupts that white pacing. The man takes his dinner, and his greatcoat from the hedge, and an old sack, and gets round under lee of a bank, and makes a seat for himself in the dead grass. I watch him enviously: I think of what food and drink there is in that basket. Some fat bacon perhaps between two wedges of bread, or a bit of cheese and a raw onion. The bottle I suppose contains tea, that ought to be beer. My

mind goes out hungrily to coarse food eaten on a couch of dead grass in
the March sun. One becomes preoccupied with food. Lying dry in the
mouth I have been obsessed since the pain abated by the thought of a
glass of beer, longing for something clean and bitter to bring one back to
life. None of the things offered were any good: soda water – ugh! orange
drink, lemon drink; they left a sort of sweetness about the mouth. But
that glass of beer (so bad for a brain-ache) – again and again I drank it in
imagination. In the small hours there it stood before me: I paused with
the glass at my lips, to smell the smell of it, then drank it in one draught
– in my imagination. It was cold; it misted the outside of the glass.

Now, at the window, I watch the bottle that ought to be beer raised to
the lips, its bottom shooting the sun. The labourer is drinking to the sun
in my beer dream, a quart of it, home-brewed. It is that beer (this also
came to me in the small hours) that the miller used to brew, who ground
my corn in his windmill on top of a little hill. And when I paid him his
account he would bring out two glasses, and we would sit in his little

hut of an office and drink his beer while the mill sails came sweeping past the window, making a regular swift shadow through the room.

I think, too, of the old beer out of the stone bottles in a barn on days of rabbit shooting, gulping it down in quantities. What would I not give now for even a wineglassful. I count the days till I shall be well enough for that draught.

Now the bedroom door opens, and in comes Nora with my dinner on a tray – a morsel of steamed fish, half a boiled potato, and a glass of water.

In the afternoon another figure comes into my landscape. It is William going on to his piece of ground. I try to guess by the movements of his distant figure what he is at. First I see he is digging. Then he appears to be making long, slow, reaching-out movements. Raking I guess. Now he is bending down: he seems still and intent. Sowing something? Can the land be fit already?

The man in the Black Horse showed me how it was done with a twist of the wrists: his were more eloquent than the words. I could clearly see his father walking backwards across the field with his dibblers, dibbling holes for wheat. 'He would go very nearly as fast as you could walk: oh, acres he's done.' The twist of the wrists kept the points clean of mud. 'They shone like new steel.'

This oldish man – Saxon clear in his eyes, with fair not-yet-all-grey moustache, his drink on a shelf above him, and the little grey nervous man beside him, and I, were detaining one another longer than we had intended. It was – at last – my glass of beer. I had only looked in for a few minutes before the ride home after market against the wind. I was very busy; there never is a moment to spare really, if you have even a little land. But here I was, oblivious to the fact that the bar was noisy with townsfolk and town talk, time going on. The little man in a town suit with his big mug of stout (it is the little, nervous people you find grasping the big mugs) suddenly became animated. I had thought, seeing him first, that he was in some small indoor trade; one of those people whose lives are ground away between walls of back premises, monotonous hours upon hours, till at a certain moment in the day they dart round a corner into a usual seat in a usual pub, and are at peace. But the hands kept uneasy. In those movements that led nowhere, plucking at a button, rubbing an ear lobe, I sensed the effect of the bombage on that frame; and by the way he sat. Pinned down by all sorts of circumstance; by economics, by the war, by a sort of gentlemanly-seeming – there he was, the victim of our time. His quiet Saxon companion was classless – he might have been a pre-conquest king, or a peasant. That face going back to the days even before feudal England, with the naively delicate lines of nose and mouth, was held in a strength of stillness. He smiled out of the past. It was again the repose in alertness that is the country genius. There was something he had in common with the wind and the birds: whatever goes over or alters the face of the land, they have the freedom of it and always will. The type of men whose home is in this 'deep tender-heavy clay' as the farm auction notices call it, cannot be moved, and their mind is of its nature. Their stillness is a luminous pondering of that soil – deep, tender-heavy.

It was right that he should imbibe the golden ale. He did it royally, without hurry; harvests gleamed to me as he tipped it up. His genius was of the earth; it was simply this: that he could make fifteen rods of ground produce as much as another man's thirty. This was generally acknowledged. People came to him for the secret, as though it were something that could be had in a word, or at most, a phrase. But people are used to that form of specific – it is the whole art of advertising. He would tell them things about whatever it was they were trying to grow; but that was not the whole story; that could not be told, least of all by him, with whom it was all an absorption and second nature. Alertness in repose: watchfulness out of an experience going back beyond his own life – and the hands. The quirk of the wrists in the use of the dibbler made the other man exclaim, 'It's in the hands.' He put down his mug and began to demonstrate another act of husbandry there in empty air. So that the tool and the field were imaginatively brought before me.

Surprisingly to me – for I was right, he had a small business in the town, and his hands had for years been subdued to other uses. 'Ah' – his eyes sprang awake behind his glasses – 'I was delivering a chair I'd re-upholstered to a farmhouse. They were cutting round the wheat to let the binder in. "This here'll be something strange to you," the farmer cried. "Eh, strange?" I said, "what's the chief thing about it – to keep the heel down, ain't it?" That made him look. "Here, give me hold of that scythe and I'll show you." I mowed all round that field for him. "What – you've been in this business then?" "Been in it – I went to work on a farm when I was ten years old."'

He was proud; he was back in his Suffolk speech, too, full of deep-mouthed ejaculations of wonder and assertions of bodily power. Up at six driving bullocks that had never been out of a meadow before to market: quite alone with these cattle, chasing them around big fields and back on to the road again; till he was rewarded, at Norwich, with as much breakfast as he could eat.

His children won't believe that he ever worked so hard; they think he is putting it on when he talks in such heroic terms of the past; they can only see what is before their eyes – fields, sleepy cattle, miry yards – when they go for a country jaunt. They chaff him about it. But here he can talk and be believed, and corroborated. Able as he is as an indoor craftsman he would recover former powers; they are the real triumph over circumstance, not economic but physical. So in a measure his body awakes and almost puts on power; the nervous, empty gestures become movements of skill with seed hod and reaphook. We tell over the old tale of corn and horses and wooden ploughs. Our Saxon friend is quiet in his certainty of the completeness of those former ways to serve eternal needs. He, too, of course, was bred to farming. His fifteen rods is in the nature of the finely tapered finish of a strong shaft. Everything he has in him is in that. The shape, bloom and colour of produce is his care now, the nourishment of his life.

There is to every man an amount of ground suitable to his talents. Few know it, and most are continually striving to add field to field till they have too much. I know one who farms forty acres and no more; and he makes of that a beautifully complete thing, as productive as his neighbours' hundred acres. Another I know who had the strength of purpose to take one hundred and fifty acres when he had capital enough for three hundred – and the same again applies.

My friend of the inn with his fifteen rods also has found his measure; is complete within it and wastes none of his thought in looking beyond. It is one of the last lessons a husbandman learns – if ever he learns it – that more land does not mean more produce.

His Saxon blue frankness of eye and quietude made him a man to talk to: drinking his ale as by right, with a regalia of first-prize produce to his credit. A king of this ancient island. His neighbour gesturing much more, and protesting too much, as compensation for the indoor years.

Ale and the earth made between us three a friendship not measured by time; our corner was a festival of husbandry. And I still think of what solemn fervour that topic engenders where two or three are gathered together, and what unanimous condemnation of anything opportunist or thriftless in connexion with the land.

I still see the hands moving in air with various knacks and rhythms belonging to the work. The hands of the little man whose weakness showed the more as ale made his vehemence the greater and his gestures more ambitious – the one throwing into relief the other.

And though we talked long and loudly, the hands still retained something that no word could catch, moving just so and so.

'Let's go on.' We manage at last to refold the map on the windy fifty-acre common. It should be spring – March is out – but it is winter, no doubt of it. We decided to have a day off, and waited for days for a spring day such as Edward Thomas wrote of, calling it March the 3rd.

> Or do all mark and none dares say
> How it may shift and long delay,
> Somewhere before the first of Spring
> But never fails, this singing day?

Somehow a brilliant dawn uplifted us and we set out, telling each other that it would turn to rain, and hoping thereby to be proved wrong.

To start with it turns to wind. When we get, in the teeth of it, as far as the bleak high common, we say, 'Shall we go on?' Nora gets off her bicycle and I fall off mine, and we stand wondering what on earth we came out for. To have a day. We see by the map that it is as far to go home as to go on. At home a good dinner awaits us. On – and there is no knowing what we shall get. It is going to rain, too. We *will* have our day. Come on. Thence-forward we insist on enjoying it. There is at least a smell of earth in the wind. Beside a farmyard in the ruins of a castle men are threshing out clover seed. Dense clouds of dust and smoke are pouring from the tackle. It is one of the worst jobs on a farm. It makes cycling against a cold wind a luxury. A man with a felt hat gone basin-shaped, swarthy as a South American with dust and smoke, goes running across the yard as though he is chasing a rat or is late for something. When he gets there, which is leeward of a corn rick, he takes up a bottle. One *would* run to it, at that job. The massive, splitting walls of the old castle contain the threshed corn stacks like a mould of clay coming away from the new-born golden straw. The running, grimy man makes a crisis of those grey towers, his no-date hat and clothes. Yet there is something almost modern in the massiveness of the walls, the armadillo age of man upon us again, tenfold reinforced. The towers stand up tall, boastful. But today only in the thickness of the earth is there safety.

It is good to see the lace-like top of the church tower of our destination stand suddenly out of the blue obscurity beyond the hill. The uncouth castle and the wind up here have much in common – but that tower top in the vale stands still. So delicate, that if there were a wind down there, surely it would be ruffled.

We glide down, and there are crocuses in the gardens of the suburbs, and after the suburbs calm red Georgian houses of which the best always seems to belong to the doctor. Yes, there is his plate and those different bell-pushes, and a tube inviting you to yell into it. Warm, safe, happy houses with elegant porticos like frames awaiting a caller.

Only an empty stomach can ruin our day now, or a stale bun in a teashop, which would be almost worse. That is what we are really thinking as our eyes trace the nice eighteenth-century details of those houses, thoughts which the extreme though appropriate quiet of the street does not answer too reassuringly.

There are two inns, opposite each other. Of the one, the door is open, but the sheet in the glass frame on the wall which was once a bill of fare has been there so long that absolutely nothing is decipherable to our combined eyes but the word COLD in the palest of pale pink ink.

Whether, years ago, they thought when they wrote that bill of fare that the word COLD looked less cold written in red ink, I do not know. It certainly makes no impression in such a state and on such a day as the present. We try the opposite inn. This has at any rate a thoroughgoing commercial look, though closed and curtained. We penetrate through various doors into the authentic gloom of such a place. Gloomier and gloomier. Yet it feels as though market dinners might once have been eaten here, when such little towns had lively markets and needed gossip-and-bargaining corners. It is not the gloom but the silence that dismays us. The place is a labyrinth. At length Nora deciphers 'Dining Room' written backwards in frosted glass. The door is hinged back, open. We enter and see an electric stove half alight. It is a miserable thing, but hopeful to us. I find a bell push concealed in the lincrusta. A large rosy girl enters: the room seems to light up.

'We should like some dinner, please.'

She departs with neither yes nor no, and we hear her imparting our message somewhere beyond a stone passage, and it being answered in an elderly, enigmatic mutter. We stand shivering till the rosy girl's return.

'It's steak and kidney pudding today and will you take soup first?'

By all means, yes, we'll take everything. I dash off one of my overcoats and begin to feel at home. There are several levers attached to the electric stove, which has also a piece of scenery purporting to resemble glowing coals, in which a mysterious shadowy motion occasionally occurs. We try the levers; but although one of them will put the stove right out none will put it right on.

But the dinner is capital: steak and kidney pudding as big as the plate, a pint of beer in a tankard as bright as silver, and a schoolboy's helping of jam roly-poly to follow.

Outside there is a great yard, and facing the window a piece of statuary in the shape of a Victorian Hercules looking as cold as a Christmas morning bather, and eyeing us, I think, with envious sadness that we have the inestimable good fortune to be alive and able to thrust victuals into us against the wind and rain.

After dinner we are in observant mood, and that leads to a discovery. You never know what England hides – the England of today. It is almost as though she does hide them, bits of her old craft, deliberately, from the modern world, as though they were a persecuted religion, by putting up a machine-made façade. These old country towns have their secrets, doors behind piles of boxes and rooms like secret drawers. I go into a boot shop for a pair of laces: it is just an ordinary modern country boot-repairer's; a man at work behind the counter, boxes of factory shoes on the shelves, rubber heels on cards, advertisements for polish. Among a jumble of things on the counter I see something that puzzles me, a shape as of a hand with cubist fingers, and a hole in the middle of it; flat. There is a pile of them; they are of sheepskin. I pick one up, curious. 'That will be a glove,' says a woman coming through a door which I had not seen before – 'when it is sewn up.'

'You make gloves?'

'We have made them for generations.'

'Can we see some?'

The woman leads us through the hidden door, and suddenly we are in a great room among the raw materials of old English life. Piles and piles of fleeces; leather lying up like stacks of elm boards. Heaps of gloves, too, large and fleecy. The woman keeps tossing one fleece after another on to the floor for us to see as she talks, and the rich, alive way the depth of wool lifts and subsides in its journey through the air is beautiful to see. They look heavy, but she does it easily, with a practised rhythm:

there is a kind of pleasure in it for her, too, in the heavy fleeces floating down, like telling over again an old story.

It is a cottage industry still surviving. The gloves are cut out in this room on a big treadle machine, above which hang heavy steel patterns. Then they are taken round to the various cottages in the district, the finished work being at the same time collected and paid for.

'One old woman, who has just given up, has made gloves for my husband, his father, and his grandfather. She said to me, "And you are the fourth generation." The woman adds with a laugh, 'She forgot that I am the same generation as my husband.'

The war has deprived her of her son, who is in the Territorials. It is likely to deprive her of her foreman-assistant, leaving her with only a boy of fifteen. The raw materials are becoming increasingly difficult to obtain; the army requires them all. So perhaps this flourishing little business of generations in a back room will be killed by the war. Not killed; it could not really be killed, for these fleeces and that leather are the materials that man will need always, whether he goes back into darkness or forward into light. That is the refreshment of standing here, watching fleece after fleece floating down, and the tiers of leather (goatskins, doeskins, too); the feeling of permanence in them.

'One like these,' the woman is saying, 'has been down for a hearthrug in front of our fire for forty years.'

I should like a leather jacket like that: it is cold enough for anything. How simple a thing clothing and warmth really is: just turn a fleece inside out. Were they so uncomfortable in old England? We, clad in our thin factory stuffs, mutter about their 'terribly draughty old houses'. What could a blizzard do against that, let alone a draught? Why have we made such a complicated and finicky business of dress?

I buy a pair of gloves; thick fleece inside and stout hide out. And the fingers are not merely lined with strips which curl up, as most factory gloves are, but are sewn fleece all round. The best five-and-sixpence-worth I shall get for many a long day.

'I don't put them in the window,' the woman says, 'because they get so dirty.' Outside, attached to the shop, is a small eighteenth-century house. Yet it is nothing but an ordinary 'Repairs while you wait' sort of shop to look at. Even when you know what lies in the background, you can find no clue to it in the window. If the factory age passes in the bomb explosions, will hundreds of such village industries come out of such hiding places, and carry old England on?

By now rain is added to wind. We bustle ourselves up in capes over our coats, and start homeward. We ride five miles along a Roman road, the storm three-quarters against us, yet still have breath, somehow, to talk. Still can notice the chestnut boughs with buds bursting, threshing the air, and small farms full of hopeful preparations for the season. When we turn off that road, we turn away from the wind, and sail the last two miles.

Decidedly – especially over tea – decidedly we have enjoyed our day. To return home is like coming to a children's party. It is their after-tea playtime. Martin is throwing balls about. He takes a new plate with a picture on it we have bought him, and prepares to throw that too. Is distracted in time by Anthea's memento, a bracelet of gold; of gold paper over chocolate, that is. After a suitably brief period as an adornment, it is stripped, broken, shared, and eaten.

The arrival of a hen and eight chicks, a toy woolly elephant, and a pair of little blue shoes on a Sunday morning are a delight to Anthea. Only to us, who know what they represent, these gifts are tinged with sadness. It is nothing less than goodbye to Geraldine, Anthea's first friend. She has been sent to a safer region than this near the East Coast; her mother will follow shortly, their house will be shut up. Geraldine's father is fighting in France.

Anthea, luckily, is too young, not for affection, but to know the meaning of parting. Geraldine is of an age between Anthea and the twins. Of afternoons the walk was 'Geraldine's way' – and Geraldine's walk was 'Anthea's way'. So they would meet and go together, Anthea walking beside Geraldine's pram and, as spring came on, picking primroses and violets from the hedgerow and giving to her – picking whatever she demanded from her enthronement of white fur. Toys used to be exchanged 'till tomorrow'. Geraldine came to tea; Anthea went to Geraldine's to tea. It has been a friendship of a year or more. At first Geraldine was hardly more to Anthea than a pretty, alive doll. But a doll with all her own things – exciting. Then she gradually learned to speak, could articulate 'Anthea'. The first winter she only crawled. Anthea, when she went to tea there, took off her shoes and crawled, too – as delighted even at her age to grow younger as older. By summer Geraldine had learned to walk. She trotted about our place in a muslin frock, in little blossomy gusts of movement, Anthea following, and every now and then hugging her ecstatically. Even a painful sting was borne with fortitude in the pleasure of Geraldine's company. But when Geraldine, who had had enough of embraces, suddenly bent down and bit Anthea on the wrist, that was rather surprising. Anthea did not know what to make of it, unable to see that it could be anything but affection, although it hurt. She went very red: Geraldine was detached from her arm. There were the little indentations of teeth in the flesh, just where the sting was.

'It's all right, dear, Geraldine didn't mean to hurt you,' we began with our quick parental technique of appeasement. But Anthea out of her innocence had the inspiration.

'Geraldine was kissing my bump to make it better.'

'Of course.'

In the snowy winter Geraldine looked like a snow princess with her delicate skin framed in a white bonnet. Her elderly nanny was like a godmother in a fairy tale. In fact it was all like a fairy tale – the children meeting in the bare country featureless with snow – their bright colours the only colour – Anthea in red, Geraldine in white, trustful and happy in the savage cold. It was to me, passing them, a glimpse of that other world of the candle exposed to the wind and the bud to the frost, and the survival somehow of both flame and flower – the world of miracle beyond all those fears that make us people of experience tremble.

No illustrator of the inherent story could have painted more doomlike significance into that snow, the which stood in our minds for cold burial of all that was warm in life. Geraldine's father was on guard in it somewhere: it was the pause, we knew, the lease of calm before the earth wakening to life should bring resounding death to thousands of men, women and children. Yet one listened to overhear Anthea and Geraldine's conversation as it were to comforting wisdom.

'She calls them,' Anthea cried to me, stretching out her hands in gloves with flowers worked on them, 'my daisy gloves.'

As spring came Martin and Sylvia grew to take a part in the friendship. Martin, who sat facing forward in the twin pram, would be the first to spot Geraldine, and would make noises of delight. Geraldine, too, would cry 'Martin'. There came a great day when not only Anthea but the twins were to go to tea at Geraldine's. It had to be a fine day, because there was no way of getting there but walking.

Anthea admonished the twins – Martin particularly, who likes throwing things about – 'You must be careful of Geraldine's toys because they are precious.'

But unfortunately the day turned out wet. 'Perhaps it will be fine this afternoon,' Anthea said. But no. It had to be announced after dinner that the party was off for the day. There was a red-faced effort to master tears, which was successful – and thereafter a philosophic cheerfulness that 'another day it will be fine'. But unfortunately again that other day also turned out wet. And yet again. The devil seemed to be in the weather. Until 'all going to tea at Geraldine's' became almost one of those fantasies in the no-time of the future, like going in a train to stay with cousins in London, playing with Martin and Sylvia by the seaside when they are big enough to make sand castles. However, the day came at last. Anthea set off for Geraldine's at a great pace, adjuring the twins not to spill their milk – certainly not bubble in it.

And now that spring is here Geraldine has gone. We have instead a brood of chicks that Geraldine's mother wanted to dispose of before leaving the house, a pair of shoes that did not fit Geraldine very well, and would they do for Sylvia? And the parting present of the jumbo. Geraldine, we say, has gone for a holiday. All the children stretch out their hands simultaneously for the jumbo. It is taken for the walk – the walk today is 'the other way as we shan't meet Geraldine'. Anthea helps feed the chicks afterwards, and is surprised that they are not yellow like those of ours, but dark brown.

'Look – the mummy hen is showing them how to feed,' I point out.

'She's not a mummy hen – she's an Anthea hen.' Anthea examines the coop. 'I have a house like that – the Other House – where I and Martin and Sylvia live all alone, and I do everything for them. There aren't any big people. No.' She gives her little shake of the head.

'Why, Father, there's one of the baby chicks standing in the dish of its food!'

'So it is. Fancy if Martin stood in the middle of his dinner.'

The idea, so extravagant, slowly forms a picture. It is the cream of farce. She begins to shout with laughter.

So – it is bedtime once again. I hear the idea being retailed with more laughter, as I gather up the box the chickens arrived in, and fold up the string, such a generous quantity of strong-looking string which I put in my pocket for use about the place. Though even then I shall have qualms about using such good string to tie up sacks.

The first of May has come, and now is going, this lovely day that dawned with a mist and burst early into sun. Here at least it has been allowed to pass in hope and happiness. In the news this evening is the announcement that it has passed off 'quietly' abroad. Meaning no class-war processions in the cities. Its significance has dwindled to that.

It passed off 'quietly' here, too. Nothing has happened all day, which has become a positive blessedness. The day, thronged with associations of old merrymaking, is like a door half-open to illimitable treasures and powers; the power of the fountains that live in every natural thing, for which the world's preoccupations are too grave. And yet there are wonders at hand to draw the world even out of the abyss, if it could look. The movements of a grey warbler amid the plum tree clotted with blossom. That tiny bird moves with the silence of a shadow, in his absolute absorption in his moment. Lithe, silent, with a mouse-like quality about his greyness: feathers could not be moulded to so delicate an outline, surely.

How sharp the feeling of this Suffolk seaboard country; spring coming all in a rush, blossom spreading over it like a great splash of foam. Days disturbed by their own swift fullness, when every morning, waking early, one's spirit feels like an athlete crouched at the starting line. How one must wake sharply out of the snow to meet it. It is the country of the hard nerve, the cheerful shout, the wind-wet eye. The country of stout victuals and long-sightedness, of slowness, too, not impatient of the great to-be-ploughed tracts.

Our high farming land seems to ride the spring gale like a ship in trim: everything is neat and hoed and short silky green. But down towards the wood, crab apple trees lean out and scatter their blossom among the tidy bean rows. Here, too, the honeysuckle, our harmless hedgerow honeysuckle, assumes his true nature of snake, constrictor choking the young trees. Tightly, in sweet spirals it is wound round the trunk and has slept there all winter. Now its green leaves are out ahead of the leaves of the tree, and it prepares to continue its winding. Underneath the crab apple tree lies a dead stoat, petals falling upon his brown and saffron body; he looks so at peace, so out of the rush and press of spring, which becomes almost a frenzy to be born, to flee darkness and be fulfilled; while he, dark-minded little creature, lies flung out upon death as upon a last prey. And the rabbit dead in the snare there; long dead, sunken, hardly more than the grey-furred growth on a patch of meadow dung.

But down here in the bottom meadows, overhung by the wood, the air is moist and faint. The wind and the trim of the farm lose power: the tangled wood rings with nightingales. There is a thicket near, that once produced, men say, its ten sacks of corn an acre for them. And a house stood there, a farm of many acres. None can thrust through that growth today. A tractor began to pull the bushes up last autumn. The scene looks like a trace of giant combat; quagmire and earth threshed up and torn roots. Then the tractor gave up. Men build sea walls against the erosion of the waves, and every now and then the storms batter through them and more of the coast crumbles down. Great walls of labour – of yearly labour, desperate and short-handed – are built against the thicket bursting and pressing outwards to the farm. Invisible walls of hedger's hacking arms and ploughman's plodding to and fro.

The rabbits are the advance guard: they rush out and devour the fields. The men are busy now putting up the rabbit wire that the snow beat down. Their hammer blows echo among the trees.

In the bottom meadows an old willow, fallen and re-rooted, looks monstrous. It is leafing in defiance of its own deadness. A cow, broken away from its herd, is wandering there, lowing and running and stopping, wanting a bull. She runs into a pond, and the water is infected by her trouble and splashes about and flings the peaceful white water flowers into a tangle, and heaves green scum upon a posy of primroses. The cow comes out and stands glaring. Clouds of mud continue to move upward to the surface, and all the clear, flowered, and grassy water line is marred. The cow sinks into the mud as she stands, her sharp flint-smooth hooves cutting through the dry crust. She heaves awry, like a wreck, extricating herself: the deep mud hisses and sighs. She is bony and wild-looking. Now she stands accusing me. My passing through the meadow works on her. She goes into narrow places and rears out of them, with snapping timber: she runs into gates as though they were not there. I leave her sharpening her horns against the monstrous fallen willow. Rides have been cut through the wood. The older ones are closing in. Now I am in Chaucer's England, and all the mystery of medieval travel is present to me. In clearings there are encampments of primroses; great companies and rejoicings of them. The nightingales vibrate like light, the midday song of nightingales. Old dead trees lie fallen, weathered and grey, and young birches rise in the clearings.

I remember how the old farmer loves a wood. It is a relaxation to sit here and watch the wildness, after a day of order and cultivation; to exercise the power of stillness, that the wild things may come near. There is a pleasure in a well-kept oak wood, and also in the farmer's little island of wilderness – his plantation. This is a long-neglected estate wood, and here I am in awe of the old, old England, and feel the spirit of the island abbeys, forest-islanded each from each, rejoicing to be alone with God.

How inevitable it was that the old imagery should be potent. How could *The Pilgrim's Progress* have failed to be written in such a world? Think of this wood going on and on, covering the land, and at once it becomes more than wood – wonder and fear, the depth and mystery of the soul.

The valley of the shadow: but the primrose is potent there: and in the deepest forests of thought nightingales sing at noon.

Anthea's best day – and the world's worst. The Germans blasting their way into France – Anthea waking early and telling the twins, 'I'm four years old today.'

For weeks she has watched the tulips growing; for I told her her birthday was when the tulips were out. Tulips were in a big bowl in the room when she was being born. Yesterday, the sun's warmth opened them all again. 'Go to sleep, babies,' Anthea said, 'and make tomorrow come quickly.'

This is for Anthea her first real birthday – understood and looked forward to. Standing under the apple blossom, where bough leaned down low enough for her to reach, she smelled it drawing with her young arm at the aged bough. She fingered the newly opened leaves, their perfect forms backed with sparkling hairs. 'Aren't they beautiful?' So she stayed, holding in her other hand her bunch of cowslips.

Her excitement is quieter, but more intense than I have yet known it. That this is a day to be made much of, is the feeling of it. One almost forbears to turn on the news, seeing her passing across the landing, shining down with so whole a happiness as seems to quench the announcer's words like the sun a fire. A strange duality – world fury and luminous joy: dream touching nightmare in Nora and in me: parenthood in sharpest sense: no animal, no bird watching a cat could bear it sharper.

After breakfast, presents. A toy wheelbarrow which both babies try to take possession of, a handle each, leaving Anthea nowhere. A painting book with coloured copies of flowers. Later, when I ask Anthea why she has coloured the leaves of a marsh marigold black, she replies, 'Because it's winter still.' 'Winter?' 'Yes, in the picture it is.' Another scene, figuring a large snowball, is coloured a sad sort of green. 'Well, you see,' she explains, 'I had such a lot of green left over.'

Another present is a watering can. This I am glad to see, for I have been wanting that can for my seeds for weeks past; my big one having so coarse a rose it knocks the seedlings down. Nora, being practical and economical, as any countryman's wife needs to be, saw that the size of watering can I needed was almost a toy. Light enough for Anthea to handle, anyhow. So she conceived the idea of getting it as a present for Anthea's birthday. Anthea is proud to let me borrow it: it adds to its importance for her. The only trouble has been that I have had to wait so long for it. To know it was lying wrapped up there in the cupboard was very tempting when fragile seedlings were just breaking through.

Martin possesses himself of the watering can, and looks as though he would like to know what it is for.

Another present – the most successful of all – is a wheelbarrow load of sand from William.

This is joyful; and Anthea with her wheelbarrow and watering can busies herself all morning among it in a play that is half horticulture, half cookery. Cookery wins in the end with a selection of ornamental sand buns, and a pie of which I am told I can have 'just one slice' for dinner.

I am hoeing the beans. William is working here too. He tells me the news as heard by him on the one o'clock radio – mostly a catalogue of bombings. Again the incredible phantasm of the world over the horizon builds itself, while the gusty air makes green shadows move over the grass. I cut off a bean, and thereafter concentrate on what I am doing. The bean sacrificed to a thought of bombs reproaches me. To live in the moment of tilth and young green; to do the good one can is the best

one can. And to hear Anthea's voice babbling out of the house like a brook. I was early in the orchard this morning, waiting for the kettle to boil. I paced in the dew among the apple blossom fallen all round the tree. Alone with the sun in the garden, feeling it warm on my shoulder, and everything at its beginning. Suddenly, as at moments happens, the oppressiveness of the world tragedy left me and I listened to a bird calling from a tree and being answered from far off. It had the nature of solo and chorus, the few single notes and the distant many.

This afternoon Anthea goes with Nora to pick some tulips for her tea party. This also has been since morning a treat in store. Tulips all out and swaying on their stalks are so eminently pickable, so tempting. It has been difficult to refrain. Soon Anthea has a sheaf of them, a great goblet-glow of them, more and still more. She is allowed to pick some herself: she is very careful to follow instructions and pick them with long stalks. Later, when the twins are playing on the lawn, Sylvia happily plucking daisy heads – 'No, Sylvia,' Anthea cries, 'this is how you must pick them. I'll show you,' and tries to pick a long stalk to a daisy.

William, who up till now has regarded the war with the detached, rather tired view of one who has been through all that before – now that the Germans are on the old battlefield and all the familiar names of the past come ringing on the news, is thoroughly aroused. He and the ex-servicemen of the village are like old war horses snorting and pawing the ground. 'Why,' his wife exclaimed, after he had been assuming the role of adviser to the generalissimo of the Allied Forces, 'I believe you'd go back there if you had a chance.' 'I shouldn't mind,' he said. 'I'd know my way about.' Every day he comes with new strategies, new interpretations of the situation as announced in the news. He has a contempt for people who are ruffled by news of retirements here and there. 'Why, that was happening all the time in the last war, only there wasn't all these wireless bulletins and you didn't hear anything about it. If people had known at home all that we knew, why, they wouldn't have had an hour's sleep. Why, we hadn't hardly any shells for our guns, our rifle ammunition was half duds like the shells. The Jerries used to cheer each time a shell came over and didn't explode. They ran right through us – there wasn't anything to stop them. Only they got out of hand in the French towns looting. That's what saved us.' William seems to have a belief in Providence, plus something about the British Army which acts in despite of politicians, generals and all big-wigs. Perhaps just the fact that it is British.

A sudden humming noise. 'It's only an aeroplane,' Anthea says, as we look up and see one of England's battle planes sailing over at two or three hundred miles an hour – and she stoops again to make another sand pie. Aeroplanes are not very interesting birds, Anthea thinks. Not as interesting as the blackbird sitting on five eggs in the hedge. They don't lay those pretty blue eggs – no, nor are they as awe-inspiring, rather frightening, as that still, tail-cocked, beak-cocked bird in that nest, with the intense bright eye, that stares so coldly at a small girl who has been taken to see it.

Nora gets the birthday tea, while Anthea waits outside the door, not to be admitted till all is ready.

There. The door is thrown open and Anthea enters to take possession of her tea table. What a gallant little cake it is, a white fort with four transparent flags of flame. They have such a busy look in the breeze from the window, such a morning-of-the-tournament look. The twins point to them. Of all things that are pretty, a flame most attracts the infant eye. A flame more than a flower – more than moving water. Even a small, sun-transparent birthday-candle flame. There are also iced biscuits; and another cake which should have been the birthday cake, but it turned out too heavy. The mystery of that heaviness is to recur as the cake recurs at teas. Was it the oven? Or was it that in answering a question of Anthea's Nora lost count of handfuls? I say it is a good cake anyhow; but that won't do. The mystery is solved later. Grandmother, when she closed her house for the duration of the war and came here, brought with her many supplies – among them tins of ingredients labelled this and that. Nora went to one marked Baking Powder for her cake. When Grandmother returned from another visit she said, 'Oh, but that's ground rice. I know it so well I've never troubled to change the label.'

Nora laughed at this, but I assured her that it is the normal development in a household. You set up house with everything labelled and in its right tin; but after a time you find that the rice tin is too big and the sugar tin too small and you swap them. Thereafter for Rice you read Sugar, and Sugar for Rice. This sort of thing multiplies, till only the housewife knows what means what. Grandmother was quite surprised that Nora did not know that Baking Powder meant Ground Rice.

The sound of guns from across the sea grew louder, became continuous day and night. Nora's parents returned from a visit to London with anxious faces. We were so busy with children and the land that the war still seemed extraneous. Even in peacetime we had been used to practice gun-rumblings from the sea. A cousin in the Intelligence sent Nora an urgent message to take the children away from the East Coast. Her sister wrote, offering shelter in Westmorland. Another, more urgent, message came from the cousin in the Intelligence. Suddenly Nora and I found ourselves faced with a decision. It had not crossed our minds that our home was in a danger area: it looked so peaceful, the crops growing well in spite of the drought, the fruit trees crowded with blossom; our neighbour, Mr Brett, going to and fro with his cows as usual; Mrs Brett fetching them home with a green branch in her hand, singing as she went.

We paced the home paddock, among the cowslips, Nora saying, 'Must I take them away?' I saying, 'Dash that cousin in the Intelligence, I suppose he must know.' If we did nothing now and the children were harmed we should reproach ourselves for ever. We vacillated all that weekend. We went to market: the square attitudes of the farmers reassured us. They had always stood like that in the street, talking. They went on talking, despite a bawling propaganda van imploring them not to give way to panic. They were talking of crops, of course, and the propaganda voice, sounded much more panicky than they.

The same heterogeneous goods, and the same variety of people; from a van-load of bullocks to a smallholder's bicycle with two hens in a box. Ragged-haired, smoke-cured complexions beside fair, clean-shoed young gentlemen farmers. A man with a week's beard, standing in his pig float in a fierce abstraction; a tall, scholarly-looking person hugging a rusty mincing machine he had bought for a shilling. Our Miss Archer almost too late with a consignment of her fluffy goslings.

The auctioneer's rostrum is a vehicle like a caravan, open at one side, well-weathered. After each lot, 'Gee up!' and the horse pulls auctioneer, clerk, and one or two large friends forward to the next lot.

'What's that you're all looking at?' cries the auctioneer, popping out his head.

'Some airy-planes: they're turning somersaults up there,' one shouts.

High overhead they zoom, making curly white trails in the sky.

'Well, as long as they stay up there what does it matter?' The auctioneer returns to business. 'Now, what have we here? Ah, something pretty good. How much for a start?'

One of his friends comes out of the door at the back in answer to some remark from below. He descends and looks at one of the front wheels. 'That's all right, guv'nor,' someone else says, poking the thing dangerously, 'it's got a good tyre.'

The big man gets back. 'Gee up!' The slow ride proceeds.

Far away the loudspeaker could be heard still bawling its warnings against panic.

Here Nora and I felt fortified. Foolish that we had let ourselves get worked up into such a misery of indecision about the children going away to Westmorland. Good old Suffolk for us. We bought a calf, a roan one. It came from a neighbour who made it a rule always to send everything to market. So it went there and back.

As we arrived home Anthea was in the orchard gathering up fallen petals. 'I'm making pies for fairies,' she said.

The radio was on: through the open window I heard that the news was worse. Added to the news was the announcement that all schoolchildren were to be de-evacuated from our East Coast fringe.

Once again Nora's mother asked anxiously: 'Have you decided what to do?'

We paced Nora's flower garden, faced with it all again.

There came a day of packing of boxes. And in the evening, even more unreal, we planted out some aster seedlings in Nora's garden – simply because they needed planting out. And one morning a car appeared, and in a minute had whisked, it seemed, my whole married life away.

Leaving a few toys lying about the garden; and under the apple trees six neat piles of blossoms – pies for fairies.

In the interval which followed, life for me consisted chiefly in letters from Nora and an occasional visit to her. For the rest, immersion in seasonal tasks. And late on summer evenings, an hour reserved for tending her garden, which was all I had of her. The asters flowered and died unseen by her. After a while I ceased to move quietly about the house after children's bedtime. I returned to the sort of life I lived on my first little farm twenty years ago. It is sufficient to record that the time passed. Nor will I go into details here of Nora's life in Westmorland, of how, as winter came again, she was snowed up alone with the three in a faraway cottage, and had got to her last bucket of coal before help arrived. Sufficient to record that the time passed and the family at last returned. Almost a year after their departure, the six-thirty train which I see daily pass became of great importance to me. I visualised four faces turned this way. Within a quarter of an hour the door burst open, and the children, a year older, were running about the house again, and in and out of Ada's arms spread in welcome.

EIGHT

Double summer time

WE WERE HAVING TEA under the big apple tree that looks and is a main support of our place. Its apples are a long-keeping kind, and we rely on them from Christmas onwards. Around us our growing chicks darted after insects. We were discussing the setting of another batch of eggs: we were scanning the green depths above us for signs of apples and seeing few. When I looked down again I had an eerie feeling: my chicks had become very, very tiny. I said to Nora, 'Am I dreaming or do our chicks look very small?' She looked. 'You are right. What has happened?' Then a hen appeared, but a strange hen, with a whole brood. She saw us and began to retreat in panic.

'Where have they come from? The nearest farmyard is fields away,' Nora said. 'We want another brood.' There they were as though hatched by our imagination.

I flung crumbs which arrested the mother-bird's retreat. 'But they must belong to somebody,' I said. 'We can't just collar them.'

'The owner might sell them: they must be a stray lot. Anyhow a rat will get them if we don't, and – oh, do let's try to catch them.'

They seemed a gift somehow, appearing suddenly through the hedge like that; and questions of legal ownership were in abeyance, while, with elaborate strategy, we tried to induce confidence among them preliminary to an attempt to catch them. I had already used up the remains of the bread and butter, which could do no more than keep the hen from hurried departure at the sight of two large humans rising up a few yards away. Anthea was engaged in making a daisy chain, and this, after a glance at the chicks, continued to absorb her. We were glad, as young enthusiasm at that moment would not have been helpful.

The daisy chain was to adorn my wide-brimmed rush hat – a great shillingsworth – which Anthea thought too plain about the crown. The hat had caught on a branch as I got up, and lay on the grass near the chicks. I was throwing the last crumbs, and called to Nora to fetch me some chick food. I had only a very little, and it was precious these days, but I thought it worth gambling with a handful or two. It came just in time: the hen was calling her brood to her, 'There's nothing more here; let's get away from these monsters.'

But the chick food brought her cautiously advancing again. By slow degrees we got some wire netting round on the hedge side of her, and I tried to entice them all into a ring of it which could be closed at the right moment. I began to doubt whether rats would get them if we did not; they seemed too wary for rats. Just so far would they come but not an inch farther; and the mother hen could only be distracted by ever more frequent scatterings of food from a growing suspicion of encirclement. The chick food I was expending made me more and more anxious to get them.

We thought. We gained time for thought only at the expense of chick food; so we thought quickly. 'We must get them into the yard,' I said; 'we'll never catch them out here in the open. Get the fruit netting.'

We contrived to get a barrier of fruit netting stretched between us behind them, and they were being urged willy-nilly yardwards. At this moment Anthea rose up from under the tree, her daisy chain completed.

'Father,' she called, 'it's ready to put on your hat.'

'You must wait,' I said, in a kind of stage whisper. The hat was still by the chickens; it lay there on the grass.

'I'll get it,' Anthea cried.

'NO – don't move.'

'But I've been making this daisy chain to go on it.'

'Wait,' I hissed.

'Oh, but I do want to put the daisy chain on your hat.'

The chicks were circling the hat; found it inedible. The hen boggled at it.

'But, Father —'

'What?'

'It'll be bedtime in a minute.'

The obstacle of the hat is still not passed, but we are now quite close to the yard. We slowly make the netting into a half circle round the gateway. Anthea stares at our precautions.

Mrs Richards, our evacuee, appears at the back door, and seeing that Nora is engaged, offers to bath Anthea. Loud protests from Anthea, which nearly cause the hen to take to the air. 'But, Mummy, I haven't put the daisy chain on Father's hat, and you promised me a story before bedtime.'

Mrs Richards's daughter appears. 'Oh, some more dear little chicks!' She runs forward with a sort of wide and general embrace. Our frantic gestures halt her, and she shrinks back precipitately, wondering what awful change has come over our usually cordial selves.

Anthea has calmed down, and stands patiently watching our antics.

'Mummy,' she says, after a long silence.

'Yes, dear?'

'You know, I don't think you will be able to do what you are trying to do.'

The critical moment has arrived. The hen sees the trap, and with a wild squawk comes hurtling back.

'We've got her,' I cry.

There is a rending: the hen goes flying clean through the netting: all we have caught is one chick, and that inextricably. The squawks of this chick which we try to untangle are added to the pipings of panic from the lost others, and the fury of the hen who returns and buffets us with her wings. Extraordinary the fracas that one hen and chicks can cause when thoroughly upset. The hens in the field take up the tune; our own chicks run hither and thither: the pigs gallop round barking: the geese honk and hiss. We give it up. Our only desire now is to restore peace, and her chicks to the stray hen, that she may lead them off through the hedge whence they came. But will they be restored? Not a bit.

'Where are they, anyhow?'

At last we locate the squawkings: two in the stable, and the rest deep in the interstices of a ton of coal. There is nothing for it but to wait. We go indoors, picking up the hat and giving it to Anthea. She wreathes her daisy chain around it. That at least is satisfactory.

'I didn't think you'd catch those chicks, you know: and now they've lost their mummy.'

Presently we see seven sooty atoms creep out from the heap of coal, and leg it for all they are worth out of the yard.

'In practice it's not so easy,' somebody said, 'to live simply.' We were sitting in a little mill house among paddocks, having supper with Brenda and Jane who run a smallholding. Before the war Brenda was a head buyer in a London store. Copper pans on the west-facing wall blazed in the setting sun. The hayfield outside had a rosy crest of sorrel, and the flowering grassheads glittered. Then the rook appeared, stalking up the path. It was a tame one, rescued after a farmers' battue, found lying in the grass, its flight feathers shot away on one side. He stood peering in at the door saying: Here I am.

'Meet Joe,' said Brenda.

Joe spends the day in an apple tree, or if it is too hot, in the garden shelter. He climbs upon the garden wall opposite the front door to be fed, flapping up a little ladder put there for him. His perky eye contradicts the faint pessimism (vaguely Victorian-clerical) of his down-turned beak. Bread and milk is dropped into his open maw, and, for second course, laying pellets which fall rattling into his gape like beet seeds down the funnel of a drill. And he makes huffing, chuffing, squelchy noises in gratitude, or complaint, according to whether the food is to his liking, offered in the right sequence, or whether it's 'Enough of that: now I want my bath.'

He has a twice-daily bath, in fresh water poured into an old milk pan on the wall. He will not bathe in stale water. Then he is taken up and launched into the air, whereby he can flap himself into the branches of the apple tree five yeards away. Towards bedtime Joe flops down from his tree, then up the ladder on to the wall, and from thence down upon the grass on the other side, and so along the path to the door of the room where we sat at supper. Joe is given his supper, followed by a drink. He only drinks at sundown, and that drink has to be milk and water. Neither pure water nor neat milk will he touch – nor any bread and milk left over from yesterday. Such epicurean habits can a foundling rook acquire in six weeks.

He talks all the time in basic squelchy syllables which express a variety of emotions. His benefactress has discovered their meanings, since the same utterance is repeated till the thing wanted is produced. Joe looks for a spell of petting before he will settle on his perch – which is the brass-knobbed rod which controls the damper of the wall oven. He makes little vibrations of pleasure, a sort of purring, while he presses his plumage against his mistress's neck and has his throat and back stroked. Finally he is given four brass buttons threaded on a string looped over his perch, and tied with a double bow or knot. His evening game is to unravel knots with his beak, until the four brass buttons fall to the floor. Then, and not till then, he settles for sleep.

So I could see what they meant when they said at the mill, 'It's not so easy to live simply – even in a cottage in the country.' For there was a robin waif too, hardly fledged – perhaps turned out of its nest by a cuckoo. It was found lying on the roadway among speeding cars. Rescued, it too became imperious, and demanded food at hourly intervals to the minute, delivered on the tip of a paint brush. It has just been weaned to a diet of chopped worms. Worms take much deep digging to find in this hot weather. Where do parent robins find them?

And then there was the matter of a windmill to be demolished. I had watched it for the last twenty years slowly becoming a skeleton; its sails, a ragged cross against the sunset, looked like the martyrdom of Merrie England. Restoration was too costly: the mill became dangerous. Yet how tenacious its timbers were when men came to dismantle them. The millpost was as sound as on the day it was raised. The field from which that great tree was taken is still known as Millpost Field. Its top was rounded and polished with friction like the stump end of a huge iron bolt. It fitted a socket in the main beam and turned in it, wood turning against wood for centuries, lubricated through a hole a foot long drilled obliquely into the beam. Eight different woods had gone into the making of that mill – apple, pear, elm, oak, ash, deal, pine and hickory.

And when it was down, and the whole of that subtle structure was an incoherent mass of timbers lying in the grass, there was found tucked into a mortise of the main beam, that had stood high in the top chamber of the mill, a letter from the sweetheart of miller dead and gone a century ago.

This, then, is a specimen of the simple life of three acres and cow (or, in this case, sows) in the heart of the country, where nothing, of course, ever happens.

I lunged at a monstrous group of nettles, and my scythe fell to pieces. You do not realise how many pieces of a scythe there are to fall and lose themselves, until you are looking for them among a mass of nettles. And every hook and peg a vital part of the thing: one goes and all go, and the blade swivels round and hangs useless as a broken limb.

'I never did like that stick of yours,' William said. 'That's a stubborn old bit of wood, and you've got to reach out to the work so.'

I bought it more years ago than I can remember – in those days when I walked into farming and ordered just tools – billhook, fork, scythe, saw, and so on. Thus I came by a left-handed billhook, an ungainly scythe, and by luck a good saw.

And, of course, a whetstone, or 'rub' as they call it, to go with the scythe.

'Why, sir,' the agricultural ironmonger said, 'some labourers come in here and spend a long time choosing a rub – they won't have this one because it's too heavy, and that one because it's too soft or too rough or not quite the shape they fancy.'

My hesitation, of course, had been one of mere bewilderment at the various choices in this seemingly simple matter.

Only the day before yesterday I bought another – the last one's last fragment was worn so small that I cut my finger whetting with it.

It is a stout, barrel-shaped one, cut out of the solid stone, not a made-up one which disintegrates if you let it get wet. To every man his own scythe and his own rub. Mine is a little too soft for William's complete approval. His scythe is a beautiful thing, the blade worn thin as a knife, the stick light and curved. The handles are set in a peculiar way, and no one else could scythe with them thus, because William was wounded in the last war in the arm, and yet so manages the arm that he can swing his scythe as easily as any man – he and his scythe are in peculiar and perfect harmony.

My finger is bandaged and stiff this evening, my shoulders ache. The sun is slanting low on our first day of mowing. The swathes lie like grey trails of smoke across the paddock, which looks twice its size of this morning. They tell a story – a story of two scythes – William's thin and short-bladed, mine lank with straight lank handle. 'Yours do reach out too far and push the grass across.' There the swathes show it – lying in twos where mine has thrust too closely against his. William, despite his arm, so cleverly manages his scythe that it swings around him as lissomly as the hem of a skirt from the movement of a woman's hips. My new stick is an old stick of William's that he discarded long ago, but lighter than my old one, which had split at the head, and been bound with wire, and finally fell to pieces in the attack on the nettles. Of course, I had lost everything of importance in the nettles – leathers and iron pins. But we took one from the handle and made do with a nail which he pulled out of the stable wall, and he brought from his pocket heel-shaped pieces which had come from a shoe factory – made of paper really, but looking like leather, which he finds excellent for wedging a scythe. We tried the blade this way and that way – measured its position. It should make an equilateral triangle if a line were drawn from the point of the blade to the lower handle. The handles to be the length of a man's forearm apart.

Nora brought us drink and laid it under the oak. The sun beat down.

There were marguerite daisies, vetches and many wild flowers standing in the grass. The whole art of the scythe is to watch your blade and be certain of what you are doing. Your mind must be on your work. No – your mind must be your work – mind and body one. Feel the blade swing through the grass the moment before you actually swing it – as an archer wills his arrow to the mark. I stop and sharpen twice to a journey. William demonstrates the superiority of his rub by sharpening my scythe so that it goes for the whole journey.

All goes well until I come to a stump. That is nothing to William, who yearly scythes the grass in the churchyard. He scythes right round a tree leaving not a blade of grass standing, yet not touching the delicate point on the trunk. Such things throw me out of gear, and I have to say to my scythe as it swings back and pauses a second on the verge of another cut, 'Now *you* do it – you do the work.' And the scythe like a living limb responds and comes sweeping through the daisies with sweet, even motion, while my arms are unconscious of the weight, and my eyes watch with pleasure the point swinging round towards my left boot with just sufficient force to cut the last blades and no more. I come to feel an indolence in action, letting the scythe do it, and a force that is not me takes possession of us both and we swing, swing. William ahead there, half encircling himself with his blade. 'I mow to suit myself,' he says. There is no keeping time with him. I have tried, and suddenly the grass seemed tough as wire, the scythe as clumsy as a tree. There is my time, and his time – we mow to suit ourselves.

'Ah,' he cries, 'I saw that just in time.' It is a hidden tree stump. He mows nicely round it. 'There – we can see him now.' 'Once,' he said, 'mowing just about here I put my blade into a pheasant on her nest. The young ones were just coming off. She sat so close I didn't even see her. My blade went into her. I felt my blade go into something soft, and my blood ran cold.'

William went through the last war: was blown up, buried, fought with the bayonet. But mowing into something soft in our meadow his blood ran cold.

A partridge flies up in his face suddenly, and we find the nest under the brushwood round a beech; fifteen eggs, dim-mottled, tapering. He holds one up to his ear and listens. 'Yes – they're almost hatching.'

'They'll soon be eating my peas then,' I say.

He looks around. 'No, I reckon they'll fly over the road into Mr Croft's corn to feed.'

We remark again on that other partridge's nest in a clump of poppies where the children run to and fro and play ball and laugh and shout. Thirteen eggs the bird laid there, and sat close.

We speak then of the white owl that haunts between our orchard and the churchyard. Regular in her flight, taking almost the same course each dusk: she companions our wintertime: will sit for an hour at a stretch on an apple tree here, for an hour on a tombstone near William's window; and does not move for either of us going near. We told each other, when in the spring we missed her, that she was probably sitting hatching some eggs. But now it is mid-June and we are getting anxious about her. She has been flying between William's house and mine for years. Just as it is getting dark in the winter her white motion will go threading through the boughs – breaking the day-long stillness of frost or mist.

William and I work in unison; and we have the same pauses. We enjoy the day as we work, stop to say, 'Yes, look, there's going to be some apples on this tree,' or 'There's some plum blossom set here.' Up in Westmorland, where I visited Nora just after our harvest and took a hand in theirs, they work so hard that there was hardly time to eat the big tea that comes out in the broad butter baskets, or to drink the tea without scalding one's mouth. It was, 'All right, Mr Bell, don't hurry – I know you like to take your time over your food' – after I had been gulping tea and gooseberry pasty for all I was worth. Meal upon meal, till I felt pendulous as a kangaroo.

I was impressed afterwards by the slow steadiness of Suffolk, where we can believe in tomorrow being another fine day. People passing on the road might have seen movements not obviously connected with mowing – William after whetting his scythe suddenly begins marking time upon

his swathe. He is telling me how in France he saw horses treading out the corn, and automatically his body enacts it. Now he bends forward, one hand outstretched, the other sweeping the air under it: he is telling how he watched the women reaping the corn with sickles which their men (many already dead in battle) had sown. Again marking time on the swathe: this time it is a dog treadling a churn round, slowly, slower – then the woman putting her head out of the door and waving a stick, and his feet accelerate to the double.

Now Nora is bringing tea out under the trees; but we do not stoop till we have mown right over the edge of the ditch, and I swing mine down into it. We mow off all those small shoots of bramble and thorn which start at the edge of a meadow and creep inwards. That means frequent whetting. His scythe edge is as wavy as the sea; every nick is a history of his labour. 'That one there – I did that quite soon after it was new, mowing the churchyard. There was a headstone covered by grass. I caught it properly: it took a piece right out of the blade – twelve years ago and you can still see the place.' So we walk slowly to the oak where Nora and the children sit among the swathes, and eat lettuces, and brown bread she has baked, and oatcakes, and plum cake, and drink cup after cup of tea.

'It's like making sheaves,' Anthea says, getting up and gathering the hay in her arms. Under the tree it is rank and has dried strawlike. Last year in Westmorland, where all the corn is bound by hand, she made her first sheaf, a little one; and I showed her how to bind it. Martin has hold of the hay rake and is nearly bursting himself trying to wield it like a man. The teeth are caught in the roots of the grass and he is red with vexation. I tell him he had better put it down; but William lifts himself up from his comfortable reclining position against the tree trunk and shows Martin how to hold the rake halfway down the handle to make it stand upright, and then the teeth slide through the grass. But soon he is in trouble again. 'Never mind, I'll make you a little rake, Martin, one that you can handle,' William promises.

Sylvia is carefully picking a doll's plate full of daisy heads. 'Who are they for?' I ask her.

'For Oddy-Doddy,' she answers without looking up.

'Does he like daisies for tea?'

'Oddy-Doddy's a she.'

'Oh – and does she like daisies?'

'They're plums.' The big blue hat and square printed slip of garment go sailing off into the back garden, where presumably Oddy-Doddy lives.

Oddy-Doddy is a character built up from nonsense chatter. The twins are always shouting invented words at one another and somehow that one stuck, became a person, and was endowed with characteristics. A little girl, I gather, something like Sylvia, only a good deal naughtier. Martin follows her. I find the daisy heads being given to the chickens, who waggle them in their beaks ineffectually.

Anthea stays in the hay with her child's book of ancient tales retold. Since she first learnt to read words of one syllable she has practically taught herself. Any day she is to be found sitting under a tree immersed in a fairy tale, murmuring it to herself. 'What's the story, Anthea?'

'This one's the story of Joseph – I have just finished Romulus and Remus.' She hands me the book. 'You read it to me,' she suggests.

I glance at the story. 'It's better as it was told first, in the Bible.'

'Well, read it to me out of the Bible.'

'You go and fetch it – no, the shelf is too high. I see that I have put an end to my comfortably sitting here. I make an effort to turn back to her book. 'No, you said it was better in your book.'

'All right.' How stiff I am. I go and fetch the Bible. What a tremendous story it is – I had forgotten many of the details. Wiliam is munching slowly. 'I bet that chap felt bad – Judah, when they found the cup in Benjamin's sack.' William spent some time in Egypt in the last war. 'That must be a terrible country in a famine. Now here in Suffolk we are always sure of a crop.'

So teatime passes. Already our morning swathes are fit to turn. The sudden heat threatens to parch our hay to tinder. We must cock it tomorrow.

At eleven o'clock at night I lean out of the bedroom window after supper of lettuce, fresh carrot thinnings, spring onions, and home-made cheese in the orchard, and smell the smell of the hay for the first time this year rising from those smoky-looking grey lines that stripe the meadow. It is too dark to show the marks of my blade in the grass, sign of bad work, where I lagged a little. I think only of my scythe, renewed by these days of use and shining keen again, the swing of the work, that alliance of muscle and wood and blade that is mowing.

As I build the cocks to William's raking of the swathes, we just keep up with each other and are all day at talking distance. I tell him of how in the north they were surprised when I told them we made cocks with a fork. There they use their rakes, cutting off and bundling up long bolsters of hay like Swiss rolls, and dumping one on another; a most unsatisfactory way, I thought, leaving a cock that is, as they themselves say, 'cockly'. But theirs is a grass district and ours a corn, so I thought there must be some superiority in their method I did not know of. But here, building again our big Suffolk cocks in our Suffolk way, with the fork, I am convinced that this is the right way – shaking the hay out at the bottom, and gradually building the cock, tossing the hay on lightly, not in a lump, drawing one's fork round the trailing skirt of it, and putting that on top, till the whole forms a perfect dome, whose rightness (or slight wrongness) you can only appreciate when you are at a distance of the next cock but one. I work slowly perhaps, but it is impossible not to be aware of the art of the job as you do it, and nothing less will satisfy me. I know that I shall be gazing at this field again from my window at eleven o'clock tonight, and shall hope to see something well done. What matter that the weather is set fair and all will be undone and carted the day after tomorrow? I have continually beside me the shade of the farmer who taught me, years ago, and he was a great judge of haycocks, as of every other job in the field.

The children, of course, want to cart the hay, too. William, resourceful as ever, produces for them his barrow, which is a box on an old pram chassis. This he has praised to me again and again, as though it were some costly new farming device. The King's glass coach would not evoke any higher expression of admiration in him. This object, on worn and shredded tyres, has been his answer to all his little transport problems for years. I myself have seen a great settee loaded on it, which he was bringing from a sale. When a slate blows off the roof he will bring his builder brother's forty-stave ladder along on it. It is worth more than the most expensive wheelbarrow with pneumatic tyre to him, for which I am sure he would not swap it.

Today it is the children's hay wain. They trundle it to and fro; at least Anthea does, the others pushing behind and shouting. William loads them a good load. When he has done, the barrow has disappeared, and something like a great grey sheep stands there. How children love hay, to smell it, to throw it about, and roll in it. They are happy with their wagonload.

I notice as we load and unload the hay the different scents of it. It is not all just 'hay'. And when I took a wisp to make a nest in a corner of a shed for a sitting hen this evening, I found she had a bed for her eggs smelling of wild mint.

Our little stack is finished: the weather has been perfect, the sun almost too bright and strong. Anxiety is over. Is it? How is our stack going to settle? Will it stand straight and square or – ? Yes, it is tending already to lean from the eaves. William has gone home to tea. I let mine get cold while I fetch a big pole to shore it up.

I have taken it in time: as the stack sinks, that lean is rectified. By bedtime it is trying to go over towards the side. I shift my shore against that. By the morning, what? Nora is surprised at my jumping out of bed so nimbly and so early. I really am anxious for the stack, for it is rather narrow for its height. Good, it still stands, at any rate. When I come to have a close look I see that it will always lean a little in that direction, but it is no worse; and from the road I am rejoiced to see that it appears quite straight. The roof has flattened out, and it is steaming faintly. A ripe smell comes from it: a foot inside it warmth meets my hand. The real time is half past four, midsummer morning: birds are singing all round. It will be all right. I shall have a good morning, raking the field and topping up my stack roof again to look even straighter from the road than it does. I shall fake that roof a bit.

Now to milking. 'Barbara Allen': I sing that doleful old ditty loudly to Selina, who lets her milk come quickly.

'You sound very cheerful this morning,' Nora says.

Sunday morning; the air full of roses; but it is blue cotton trousers for me. I hear the voice of my neighbour calling his cattle to milking. All the birds are singing: then the voice of the man calling, and in answer, the boom of a cow. But I, wretch, am not up yet. Up I get and lean out of the window. H'm, that's my haystack I can smell, rich in the air: the scent of a bed of roses under the window cannot compete with it. I begin

to have my doubts about it: I put my arm in again yesterday, and it was hot enough to hatch a clutch of eggs in there. 'All the better for that,' William assured me, 'it'll be brown and solid, like good bacca.' But I am not satisfied with bacca as an ideal for hay, not William's anyhow. I think hay should be green and sweet, as it was in the field.

One does notice the flowers as they come and go, even as one hurries by, even with a mind full of animal and vegetable cares. Every day there seems some new thing born, or acquired, or set upon eggs. Still I manage to get in to breakfast just as the family is seated, and Ada going the round with bibs, while Nora is finishing off the bacon in the kitchen. This morning, however, they have strawberries, which she has picked early. Half a pint of new milk each, then strawberries wet with dew, and brown, home-made bread and butter and honey. While we – well, yesterday our last home-cured ham's last slice was eaten, and Nora jagged a few ragged bits off the bone for the chickens, to flavour their wartime diet: put it through the mincer so that they should not be able to separate it from the potato, and then – this morning the mince looked and smelt so good that we ate it for breakfast ourselves.

Each child's bib has an animal embroidered on it. Each of these animals has to be offered token spoonfuls of food – porridge, strawberries, and so on – before its owner will take a bite. The result is just what bibs are to prevent. Generous relatives with a taste for embroidery might note this.

Sally is to arrive at ten-thirty. Also some people are coming to tea. Nora says, couldn't we perhaps do something to tidy the place a bit? I point out the invaluable young growth of wild white clover, where are our month-old chicks in an enclosure of wire.

Nora agreed. We both agreed that it was a pity it was not possible to have chicks or any young thing without dithery, tattered erections going up round them. First it was sticks and wire, then a box with a sack to shade it; then, as the heat increased, another bit of sacking draped on the wire, and so on. One always starts with the best intentions, yet the end is always the same. Only on Sunday morning do we wake up to appearances and say, 'Let's try and tidy things up a bit.'

'At least we can mow round the flowerbed,' Nora says. Her voice is muffled, she is already under a bush, dragging up weeds by the roots. So I tear round with the mower. But then I have to rig up a net to dry the mowings, because I cannot bear to waste even grass mowings at a time like this. The net is rotten, and the mowings tumble through. I am just on my way to fetch wire netting when Sally arrives. In the back of a car, her kid in a fair-haired girl's arms. Out of the car get father, son, daughter, Sally, and kid. The latter, only a fortnight old, is trying to feed on Sally all the way up the path. Father picks her up in his arms.

'I told my wife,' he says, 'that you would be sure to give her a good home.'

We promise this in all sincerity. We have already Mrs Richards and her daughter bombed out of London; now we have Sally and her kid.

I mentioned Sally this morning. 'What, another evacuee?' Mrs Richards asked.

'Yes,' I said, 'only this one can scratch her back with the back of her head.' Sally is doing it now, laying back her sharp long horns.

Mrs Richards's daughter Clara, who is twelve, rushes to Sally, tries to embrace the kid, who leaps into the air and frisks around.

Sally is all white, her kid too. She has swept-back horns and eyes that in bright sunlight do not look like eyes at all, but bull's eyes. All I know about goats is that they like everything except grass. The children, whose pet she is, are already offering her samples of produce: cabbage leaves, bunches of flowers, pea shucks, ivy. She eats everything; gobbles whole bouquets of marguerite daisies from Sylvia's hands.

Meanwhile I learn what I am to do; quite a lot apparently. Even keep her toenails cut. Never mind, I dare say somehow I shall still be in to breakfast at the same time. I think she will be a good way to introduce Martin to the art of milking. We all stand in the sun admiring her, and I think of Virgil's capellae. I think it would be pleasant to lead her out along the lanes, and sit in the shade while she fed and meditate the sort of things that Virgil's herdsmen used to meditate. She, white in the paddock, keenly white in the sun; and the frisking, snowy offshoot of her, bring a new note into this English scene; ancient, mythological. Already I am friends with her.

I take her late owner into my room and we chat, while his children and our children, and Clara and her friend from the village fraternise over Sally and her kid. All the while he is talking, not about farming, though he is a farmer, but about writing. How he once wrote a 500,000-word novel, how characters are born and live with him day and night – while in *my* head merely a white kid is frisking, leaping in the sun. He came up the path with her in his arms, a luminous-looking, gentle person, looking beyond into the world of his characters, his invented plots, his mind a medley of exciting imaginative things, and stolid farming ones.

'How, then, do you write?' I ask him.

'Fancy you asking me that,' he exclaims, 'you ought to know.'

'That's just it: I don't. I could not invent a plot for the life of me.'

'But' (we are at the gate again now) 'think.' He waves an arm at my house. 'A dead body lies in there. It has been raining; but no footprint is to be seen on the earth. Windows and doors bolted on the inside, mark you. Now, how did it happen? Think hard, and you will work it out. The apparently insoluble problem becomes soluble, and there is your story. All you have to do is to write it and take the money.'

I shake my head. 'I can't think how.' Sally's kid frisking around: the apparently insoluble – what was it?

Anthea and his daughter are of the same age. They are standing by the gate: Anthea has picked her a bunch of flowers. His son, an attractive freckled boy, is saying to Nora, 'Thank you for the lemon squash.' He picks up his golden-haired girl: 'There's good money in crime fiction,' he says, and kisses her and puts her in the car. 'You just think that idea out.'

'No, you do it: it's your idea.'

He looks at me and hesitates. 'As a matter of fact I've got such a lot of mowing to do.'

He departs in his car, leaving me with his murder problem. But Sally and the kid, too. How handsome they look in the sun on the green grass, the succulent green of growth after hay; and the children in their several-coloured summer garments sitting in a group under the tree. Her late owner, to show her capacity, milked her when he brought her. The milk hissed into the pail as strongly as from a cow's teats: two pints of it. It looked a lot better than 'the good money' to me, these days.

We have just tidied the garden. Suddenly I hear a fearful squawking from the hen coop in the orchard. The mother hen has turned on her chicks, now a month old; she has one trapped inside the coop; it tries to squeeze out through the bars, but has grown too fat. I come to the rescue. Immediately the chick has escaped mother hen becomes her old tame self to me. So tame has she been, that after letting her roam with her brood I could pick her up whenever I wanted and put her back in her coop. For a month she has scratched indefatigably in the earth for her young, who drew back and rushed forward in a circle in time with her scratchings; she has never swallowed a morsel of food till they have been fed, only picking it up in her beak and dropping it at their feet. Even yesterday she was doing that. And now suddenly she abhors them. Having expelled them she now murmurs sweetly to me. I detect a new note in that murmuring. I pick her up and carry her into the field she came from, and put her down in front of the hen house. It is nearly two months since she was there, but she walks straight up the plank and into a nest box. That was not her favourite nest box she remembers; she walks out of it, sees a broody hen in her favourite one, walks over the broody hen, sits on her, and lays an egg. Then she wanders comfortably round the field by herself.

I say to Nora, 'Now isn't that extraordinary?'

'Not at all,' she replies. 'After having a family of nine on one's hands for a month —'

Anyhow she has been a model mother; eager to start all over again, forgetful of the past.

Our teatime visitors arrive. One is an official in the ploughing up, ditching and draining campaign. He is sorry for the farmers in that many of them are bad farmers entirely through lack of money. The result is that they get turned out of their farms for bad farming, reinstated as bailiffs working for the government at government expense, and become good farmers.

Our friend and his wife are young. He is so responsible and so young that Nora and I feel more and more elderly as the time goes on. After tea we take a walk round, he in his unofficial capacity noting – is he? – things on Sunday which he will descend upon me officially on Monday to put right. That ditch between the meadows might be deeper, but I explain that to deepen it I should have to start about a quarter of a mile farther down, to get a fall for the water. Heavens, why did I mention that ditch? It was vanity, drawing attention to a well-laid hedge, now thickening out well at the bottom. But he looked beyond. I hurry him back with the excuse I should like his opinion of my haystack, yet taking him deviously to avoid that rough meadow into which I was about to lead the way. Once he is safely back I keep him looking at things like the tomatoes in the greenhouse, and Sally and her white kid, who are not subject to any government pressure. 'Where's that haystack?' he says.

With the directness of youth he plunges his arm in up to the shoulder, a thing which I have not done since it was first erected – because I guessed it might be getting too hot right inside, and – well, there was nothing I could do about it, so why give myself worry? But he drags out handfuls from the stack and we stare at it. 'Did you say silage or hay?' he asks with a smile.

Well, I am grateful to him really; it is best to know the worst.

They have gone. Yes, I am depressed. What a fool, to be deluded by those hot scorching days into carting my hay too soon – at my age! Nora takes my arm and accompanies me over the evening feeding; holds Sally while I milk her.

'Anyhow, dear,' she says, 'you have bought that stack of good hay from Mr Sonning and – well, we shall need some litter in the winter.'

Next morning I show William, wrenching out a handful and holding it under his nose, to have at least the satisfaction of showing that my fears were justified.

'Ah, well, there's bound to be a few sappy old bits of hogweed go a bit mouldy, but the *hay* now, solid as that is, that'll be lovely – just like bacca.'

Now the bounty of green peas is on us. Yet how few taste the full beauty of them. You cannot buy them. They are beyond price. Those you buy in shops, or have served to you in restaurants, are always 'corny', that is to say, mealy, with tough skins that flatten themselves against your gums, and your tongue is licking around for hours afterwards trying to dislodge them between bouts of conversation.

Oh, no, those are not green peas, they are carbohydrate pills, with chlorophyll addition. But the real green peas, young, almost liquescent, should not go with even the proverbial duck, nor be contaminated with any other flavour, but be eaten alone, as the French eat their vegetables – though man has never yet invented an implement convenient for picking them up.

> I stuff away for life
> Shoving peas in with a knife

says Chesterton's vegetarian. The fork is better, but you can impale only four at a time at your luckiest: as a shovel it lacks sides, and the early peas are round and run about like quicksilver. The spoon is so plebeian for the job that you can use it only when you eat alone.

As somebody said – I think it was Sylvia Townsend Warner – if you are going to keep up with your vegetable garden you must begin with a massacre of the innocents, taking potatoes when they are the size of large marbles, and peas before they bulge their jackets.

The old men of the village know what green peas are: they have spent years of patience growing them. (Odd, though, that an early pea should be named Meteor: what was in the mind of the man who called it that?) I was making haycocks with one who cared about peas. He loves his bit of ground, and burns earth to make it work better. The old men are firm believers in burnt earth, and our conversation was of the method of making an earth fire and keeping it in, until you have a heap like a miniature Vesuvius, incandescent within, but with a cool skin. One's first whiff of a morning is of one's earth fire, one's first care to see if the fire has broken the crust anywhere, and if so to seal it quickly with more earth.

To be able to gather a basket of new peas you need many things besides patience. To name a few: a broad-bladed hoe, wire netting or about half a mile of black cotton, red lead, paraffin, mousetraps, moletraps (or poisoned worms), a gun (against pigeons and jays), hazel faggots, a chopping block, a good billhook.

There are many labour-saving inventions; the dwarf pea itself for one, which 'needs no sticking'. But my true countryman says, 'I allus stick dwarf peas, else the pods lie in the dut and the slugs eat 'em, and where's the profit o' that?' I have tried substitutes for faggots, made a cat's cradle of string and bamboos and pretended it was less trouble, but the peas hated it and climbed one another instead of the string, until one windy day the whole lot fell flop, and serve me right. No, there's no short cut, no way of scamping that preliminary work with the faggots and the chopping block. My old friend undoes his faggots and appraises each stick separately, and discards about a third. The rest he tops and trims, and when his peas are sticked (stuck?) the row is as level and stiff as a horse's hogged mane.

By the time you have done everything that peas require of you, your hands and back and knees will be sore. The earth forces us to bow down to her before she will give us anything. We have been on our knees so often that we almost begin to worship her. To which the single cracked bell that has sounded week by week over the yew trees, and has been more sweet to me than cathedral chimes, has been a useful corrective.

At times pantheism has seemed an attractive creed, but Shakespeare knew where that might lead when he made Edmund in *King Lear* say, 'Thou, nature, art my goddess,' and proceed to plan the murder of his brother.

As for inventions, I always feel a sneaking sympathy for the old

Chinese peasant whom a European met carrying water in buckets from a canal to irrigate his field. A water-wheel, the European pointed out, would save him much labour. But the old man replied, 'Heaven forbid that I should interrupt the contemplation of the eternal Goodness to occupy my mind with the invention of a water-wheel!' On the other hand, an engineer told me how he had once to arrange for the unveiling of a statue in the East. Gusts of wind kept catching the veiling material, so that the electric motor failed to shift it. To ensure success on the day he hid a coolie behind the scenes. The august Personage pressed the electric button, but the coolie did the work. By contrast, what labour of inventiveness had been expended to provide me with tinned peas in a restaurant once when new peas were hanging everywhere for the picking. Meteors and Marrowfats – I think that is the oddest thing about peas, the names they have been given.

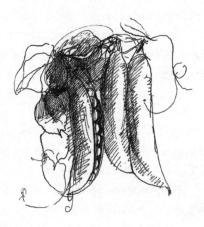

NINE

Thanks be to God

Anthea and the twins cannot understand why suddenly Ada does everything for them and they may only talk to Mummy through the window. It is impossible to explain infectiousness. For Nora has, of all things, mumps.

Of course they like to have Ada looking after them; but it would be better still to have Ada *and* Mummy. Or at least to be able to run joyfully slap into Mummy after an hour's absence shouting, 'We've been to Ada's house; we went over the stiles and what do you think we saw?' Instead of being fended off, caught, and held back like Sally's kid from Sally when we want to milk her. Trust Ada, however, to turn deprivation into a treat. The whole afternoon they spend at her house, and she makes them each a little jelly for tea. 'And we went into the church,' Anthea tells me, 'and we heard the echo' – did Ada sing a hymn for them? – 'and we saw the picture in the window; you know, inside it's got more colours than outside.'

There is only one stained-glass window in the little church, through whose graveyard one passes on the way to Ada's house. The graveyard has reached and passed its climax of growth; it is nature's garden – first of celandines and violets; then buttercups, and finally sheep's parsley. This makes a waving, misty white all over it to the height of the headstones. And now haycocks stand in the churchyard, and flank the path between the headstones as for a hay-harvest festival.

It was a sad Anthea yesterday afternoon. She tried to understand about the infectiousness, but the deprivation of touch and nearness was too much. I found her wandering disconsolately about the garden. And the extent of her unhappiness I gathered from the air of independence she adopted, answering me small-voiced in precise little phrases.

'Soon I shall be going to the post, would you like to come with me, Anthea?'

'Yes, if you aren't too long.'

'Would you like me to read you a story first from that book you have got?'

'No, thank you, I can read it for myself.' And she sits down under an apple tree and begins to read for the twentieth time the story of Cinderella. 'You go and get your letters ready for the post.'

'Well, would you just help me move the chicks' pen on to fresh grass first?'

'Yes.' She gets up and helps me shift the wire.

'There, what a nuisance. I've cut my finger on the wire.'

Often she will make a fuss just because she has been given a plate with a different pattern on it for tea. Now over the cut finger she is strangely quiet, matter of fact, saying, 'How silly of me to do that,' and turning away.

'Come – we'll bathe it.'

'Yes.' Her hands fall readily into mine now, and we go into the scullery and hold it under the tap.

'Have you a piece of rag?' I ask Mrs Richards, who is in the kitchen.

'I'll get a bit.' She comes and binds it up.

'You know,' Anthea says, looking at the finger as we walk across the fields, 'I don't call that a piece of rag: I'd call it muslin.'

Anthea can climb the stiles now, is tall enough to reach up and post the letter. She loiters in the churchyard, curious about the gravestones. We have told her their meaning; still she is fascinated. 'There's writing on them.' 'Yes – see if you can read it.' I select a fairly decipherable one. 'Elizabeth,' Anthea reads, and then after some words that the shadowless sun-glare blots out, 'Twelve years.'

'That means there used to be a little girl called Elizabeth who lived here once. I expect she played in the hay like you and Martin and Sylvia do.'

'She was a big girl if she was twelve. What else does it say?' She crouches down beside a fragrant haycock: she is eager for the written word now that she has learned to read. She has made a sudden leap in these last few weeks from words of one syllable to such difficult words as 'trouble'. Quietly, by herself, curled up in chairs in odd corners or in the garden. One day we asked her to read aloud and were startled by her swift fluency. Before then it had been 'Tom Peg has a dog', etc. I think Mrs Richards's daughter must have helped. Actually when she is reading to herself she is not reading silently. She is in fact literally reading to herself; that is, just loud enough for her own ears to hear. This, I take it, is the natural way to read, the way that people used to read, when reading was an art; because one comes across passages in old writings of someone sitting reading, and people stopping to listen. Still among country people it is the spoken word that is the reality; the written word is (what it really is) a cipher awaiting translation, lifeless without the voice.

Now Anthea crouching by the haycock is fascinated by words made in stone, channels of shadow. No doubt but the texture of the stone is vivid to her, and its weathering, the little gold blobs of lichen, and the grey, crumbled scales, and will always be part of the words she now reads, tracing them with her finger, feeling as well as seeing the shapes. 'She is not dead but sleepeth.'

'That means,' I explain, 'that when we say people die we mean that they go to sleep here and wake up somewhere else, in another world.'

This is not difficult to Anthea, for whom there are any number of worlds since she has learned to read. In fact reality is rather like a closed telescope – world within world within world, and every one inseparable and cogent. No conflict between dream and reality.

'But what's this?' she asks, staring down at a modern grave, which consists of granite stones loose inside a square curb. 'What are those stones for?'

'I really don't know: I don't think they look very pretty, do you? It would have been better if there had been flowers.'

'Or earth,' Anthea says.

We are at the stile again, but instead of getting over she sits down by a haycock. So we sit leaning against the hay and staring at the church, at Ada's house, and the two cornfields beyond already colouring to harvest; the wheat the colour of youngest oak leaves. The two best fields in the village, William maintains. And over the hedge there is the little stack of Mr Sonning's I have bought, standing among his apple trees. It is as trim as a hive, not thatched, since it is to be moved; but covered with a cloth roped well round the eaves.

'But what is that, Father?' Anthea is pointing upward to the squat turret of the church, which makes it look more like an ancient chapel.

'That's a weathercock. It is made to look like a cock – It turns, presenting itself endways –'

'It's a very thin one.'

'– and shows us which way the wind is blowing.'

She stares at its changeable motion. 'Why does the wind blow in different directions?'

'It blows whichever way it likes.'

'Did God make the wind?'

'He made everything.'

'Yes, he's the Father of everything.'

I have been surprised to find the idea of God so natural to a child. But I should not have been, the sense of parenthood being omnipresent: even an extra-large stone is a father or a mummy stone, so the idea of a parentless world is unthinkable. Anthea's natural, positive happiness in the idea made me think that heaven is perhaps nearest to a child, not in the ideal, wistful way of the grown-up, but in the quick and flashing validity of the world before its eyes.

The motion of the willow that stands over the church instead of a tower is as gleaming as a spring shower. The leaves have the soft movements of weeds under water, from which the fractured top sticks out like the mast of a wreck. Just a stark slivered trunk, motionless, rising out of the soft breathing gloss of leaves. I love that willow: I love all willows,

but that one in particular. It has the combined beauty, in its stark top and luxuriant underleaves, of the youth and age of the tree, of its winter and its summer. Especially as it stands in relation to the church – the tidal, grainy life-grey of the trunk beside the rough grey of the stone, and the elusive, flashing and flowing grey of the leaves in the wind. While there the buttress-rock of the church stands breaking the wind. And another motion of wind is over the ripening cornfield opposite, an intricate weaving of the young ears.

The church door stands open: a beam slants across the dusk inside, amid all the general effulgence treasuring light. I find in the interior of the church a counterpart of mind: the stillness is like thought.

I was drinking a glass of water, sitting in the orchard at four o'clock this morning; and as I tipped up the glass the glancing water was impregnated with the crimson of the dawn clouds. I lowered it, and watched that rosiness from outer space colouring its gleams and shadows. I felt at that moment an awe of water; I knew, not with my mind only, the gift of it, the treasure of that ounce or two of transparency glinting silver and rose in my hand.

I leaned against the oak tree where the hedge is low, and stood and watched the red dawn. And the wind came pure and impregnated from far like the water, to be answered by my own deep breath. Rooks came over, cawing as they went to their feeding grounds, and the blown motion of their wings and flight was one with the motion of the sky.

An aeroplane passed over, roaring and seeming dully to be thrashing its way. Dull, hard, straight movement across space, not flight: it cut the great harmony of the dawn but was powerless to break it. The sky grew together again after it had gone, was immediately healed and whole. 'As an arrow is shot at a mark, it parteth the air, which immediately cometh together again, so that a man cannot know where it went through.'

I saw man cutting across the cosmos with roaring thousands of horsepower, yet having not the real power of one horse, the mystery of him standing there in the meadow, biting his fetlock, then suddenly rearing his head and swinging round startled. How that sweep of dawn reduced the thousands of horsepower to tiny fractiousness. The cloudy spaces are too big, we cannot say, 'Look, what a mighty thing that plane is.' The clouds' forms are too wonderful, we cannot say, 'What a marvellous thing we have made.' But we can wonder at the lark hurling herself, tiny and singing, into the sky. The sky accepts it; the air rings joyfully to its song.

There is an inward correspondence to every outward thing: we are a firmament and have our inward sun. And even as the sun is in the seed, the radiant principle that makes it spring again towards the sun out of darkness, so the past is sown again, springs up in farther time, and fruits. The ideas, the souls, of men and women are sown in the world and spring forth by reason of their ripeness by the inner sun. This quickening cannot fail ultimately for evil, for sunlessness. Sowing and reaping within the framework of the firmament; that is the principle of our inward as much as of our outward life.

I did not purposely set out to find a philosophy of living. I have merely sat, tired physically, when the day's work is done in the field, either in my arbour in summer, or before a fire in winter, and not consciously thought. Watched perhaps a swallow on a wire, with sunned breast up there when earth is all in shadow, or a bumblebee fastened on a saffron-headed helenium, black-and-gold-heavy, swaying with the flower in a puff of wind. And some cell of me, tired with sowing turnips till the earth seemed to sway, knows the feeling of the bee clinging to the flower, swaying as it sways. The gulf of the air beneath him, and the close warmth of yellow blazing into the many mirrors of his eyes. He had been bruised by the storm, and clung there against the sun-colour in a trance to revive.

Or I sat on the stile opposite that gap in the hedge through which I always seem to see the country which the old Norwich landscape painters knew. I know it well, I walk it almost daily; yet seen through that hedge-window it takes on a bloom of blue shadow, and becomes more than itself, the spirit of England. As I sat opposite it today, a harvest wagon passed across it with high, slow-bowling wheels, my neighbour

seated sideways on the horse, and his man – or rather, his man's head –
appearing above the body of the wagon in which he sat. I thought they
were off to the hayfield, but soon they appeared in the meadow on this
side of the gap, and passed back again, wagon and man sunk in it and
my neighbour lolloping with the movement of the horse, staring at the
trees. Soon they passed again across the gap as before, across its view
of country, as though to reiterate and weave a human value into it. The
great hind wheel quite closed the window, then opened it again, leaving
a curved spray of wild roses in much the same curve as its own. I saw the
wheel shape still under the rose-spray, as the wagon went rolling away
into the fields. It returned with a load of hay, and stopped, and the men

stood awhile considering their stacking place, and the poised wild roses framed all. But mechanisation is coming in. I passed a combine harvester creeping round a field, nibbling the crop away; a straw baler ranges the stubble, dropping cubes; two men smoke in a trailer, waiting for the combine to disgorge another lot of filled sack. Muck from a dunghill is already being loaded and spread mechanically. By the end of the week the field will have been ploughed, the gate closed. That's harvest, that was. Later I saw a binder, and what a flapping, old-fashioned thing it looked, and sounded.

I came into the overgrown lane that leads to the Mill; there I was made richly aware of what time of year it was. Blackberries were red and turning black; teasels' heads were becoming crisp to the touch. Wild peppermint was in flower, bright as ageratum in a garden. Briars which in June had been graceful arches of rose, were heavy now with hips, and blown down in a tangle. Fifty years ago farmers were engaged in as competitive a battle to make farming pay as now, yet a lane like this to a child was a world in itself – and not only to a child. I wonder if farmers today have time to sit and watch fox cubs at play from a woodland seat that is the goal of an evening walk, as was the habit of a farmer I knew when the land was ploughed with horses? One farmer the other day expressed regret to me that he seemed to have little time to enjoy nature. So much rethinking has to be done continually in the light of scientific discoveries that the progressive farmer's mind is full of chemistry and the pros and cons of rival techniques.

From loitering in the unkempt lane to mending a pigsty for Brenda with pieces taken from the old windmill was an easy transition. What is a hobby? Working for pleasure. I love carpentry as long as it is rough carpentry – with the bark on, so to speak. With rusty nails, old wood, and baler wire I can work wonders. I drove home the last nail in the dark: the spark struck by the hammerhead did not last quite long enough to guide the last blow. But I felt for any sharp edges, imagining myself the occupant of this chalet, with all around evening coming on full of silence and late summer odours.

While I worked, the thrush that was reared in the cottage arrived suddenly on the wall, and took an evening feed from her tin there. She flew to and from an apple tree repeatedly. Such swift movement, so little noise: we are unused to movement without noise. The pattern of her speckled breast was vivid; the only sort of abstract art for me. The cats were sitting under the wall in a crafty half slumber.

'Kark!' The silence was torn, and Joe the tame rook came strutting, sable-gleaming and leggy. He chased the cats away, then tore a hole in a cushion of pennywort and inserted three pieces of biscuit in succession. He pecked off pennywort from elsewhere and plugged the hole, jabbing at it and smoothing it off with assiduity. He stood back and surveyed the effect. No one could have guessed where the three pieces of biscuit were hidden, then he launched himself into the sky as though he were gone for ever. The cats returned, ruffled. Now the domestic robin alighted on the wall and investigated the tin. This wall is the birds' buffet, not two yards from the living-room door and window.

Five geese came paddling, heads in air, white and proud. Though there was all of three acres, they must crowd and jostle one another, treading on one another's feet. Coming to the plank bridge over the ditch, they formed column of twos, with the odd one to lead. (Slight preliminary scuffle to decide which was to be the leader.) 'Honk! Honk!' They were away across the meadow, as though they knew their eggs were worth half a crown each in the spring.

Now four goats pass at a jogtrot, scenting hay. Happy mother sow, to have such company; and the air smelling of nettles and bruised elder where my hammer mishit. I have enjoyed being her subtenant for an hour, with my hammer and nails. As soon as she returned from the meadow she went straight to the rails I had affixed and rubbed and rubbed, as though to test their efficacy. Then she lay down, and her squealing brood pounced on her, and nuzzled her belly. She grunted at every thrust of every small snout, and wriggled and heaved. But her back was against the rails, which she seemed already to have forgotten; she seemed puzzled that she could not get over on her side in just the old place. She nevertheless slipped her vast bulk sideways inch by inch. At last ten piglets could get at their supper, and all was quiet.

The thrush alighted on the door of the sty with the faintest click of a claw, looked at the sow, looked at me, and as nimbly vanished.

Joe suddenly landed vertically on the path. He pecked away the plug of pennywort, gobbled the three morsels of biscuit, and betook himself to his roost.

There is a dusty window with green encrustations, and a drapery of cobwebs. You admire the cobwebs: you have no wish to brush them down. Cobwebs stretch entire from jamb to joist, or depend on a tool that has not been touched, by that token, for days, weeks, months. Not a thread is torn from these cobwebs: you see the window through them, and through the window a greenness of leaves. The leaning elder bush outside allows a glimpse of a cornfield; it frames a single shock of oats standing in the rain, suddenly by contrast with the close and shadowy green.

For it is raining when I come into Mr Wright's workshop, and I think of how many times in a farming life I have stood and stared at rain trickling down ripe corn stalks, turning the branching oat ear into a dripping fountain. It is on such occasions that the eye selects, magnifies: mine has dwelt on certain stalks and ears, certain stones at my feet, or flitted through the jumble of things that litter a country workshop when I have stepped in out of a downpour, searching maybe for a bolt of a certain size for the reaper, which one day must continue its interrupted journey round the field.

Look at it all, then – there are sixty years of working life in this workshop. More, for Mr Wright's father was a tradesman before him; a hundred years; a century of progress. A century of reckless expenditure of the earth's resources – except in this humble shed. Here has been conservation, readaptation. Take just the problem of tins. Rural refuse collection has had to be undertaken, because of empty tins; and costly machinery installed simply to crush empty tins flat. But this man has made a tin into a watering can, welded a neatly tapered spout on to it, given it a handle of wire, painted it inside and out. It is the habit of a century, a way of looking at things for what they may yet be worth – there is always some new turn for a thing to serve. If Mr Wright has not the right little hammer for a job; why, he makes that too.

The whole art of country wells and pumps is here: you will recognise the various parts hanging up – 'bucket' and 'clack' and flange; and long iron tools to draw them out of the shaft for repair. A certain old soft-water pump dated 1847 went wrong. The new owner called in the local tradesman. 'Do you understand this sort of pump?'

'I ought to – my father made it.'

There is a curious object in a corner, looking like two iron hands interlocked. 'I lost my blowlamp down a sixty-foot well. So I made this grapple. I got it back.'

Characteristic of a country workshop are its windows. There are usually several, of different shapes and origins. Casements, skylights, even fanlights; they all help to light the workshop. The darker green of leaves outside is fraught with sun-glints when the storm is past, and the wind shakes down drops like a heavier rain. These windows are my peep-holes into England. I never think of village England but I see that view from the workshop window – an angle of two ditches, and straggling hawthorn and elder, and a blackbird unaware of being observed.

Someone is saying something as my eyes dwell on the oat shock in the rain out there. 'That's a handy little plane'; or 'Look, there's one of the wires that came out of that old piano.' Gold-bright wire from an early piano that a woman wanted to have made into a table. But the wires would become part of something else one day. The quality of the glue which cemented the joints of that old piano is a cause of wonder. Here, again, is a stick with a spiral pattern grooved into it by a honeysuckle bine.

'I made that out of odd panes.' I hear the rattle of a lead-paned window, which is a sound not quite like any other. I turn to see: it is not a window, but a cloche like a miniature glasshouse, roof and sides of leaded panes. Another craft enshrined in this shop is that of lead glazing. Here is the machine for cutting the lead strips. 'Hard work turning that handle.'

There are a great number of old tobacco tins, each storing a residue from some transformation. The old piano being turned into a table afforded a respectful glimpse into the nature of the original maker (such dovetailing, such glue!). Those little bits of mechanism; surely there will be a use for them one day. Thought in the craftsman is a quality of the mind's eye. There may be a moment of groping for some connexion, and then – yes, he has it – those fine, tough wires are just what are needed; and there is a taking up of tins and shaking them, till one is found which does not rattle like the others: it is opened, and there they lie, coiled and bright.

There are old cigar boxes too. One of them puzzled me. It was heavy, yet seemed full of paper only. 'How odd,' I said, 'this box is full of pages of the Bible.' I read, 'Their bull gendereth, and faileth not; their cow calveth, and casteth not her calf.'

'That's gold leaf,' said the old craftsman. 'Bible gold.' Wondering, I lifted the pages, and between each page lay a leaf of gold. 'That's the best gold leaf; it always comes between pages of the Bible – I don't know why. We always know it as "Bible gold" in the trade.' He showed me the fine, badger-hair brush used to pick up the gold leaf; fingers were too clumsy.

Outside was his cottage garden. The cottage, the workshop and tool shed formed a square within which were runner beans and rosemary, potatoes and phloxes, an apple tree, and a bush of heavy, sweet-scented roses. Within this rectangle, a man had worked for sixty years, taking up where his father had left off. By modern standards, it had been a narrow compass; yet when I think of those green peepholes into the surrounding country; the hawthorn and elder, the blackbird and the cornfield; I revert in mind to the oldest ambition in the world, expressed in the oldest book. 'Every man under his vine and fig tree.' Bible gold.

Opposite Mr Wright's workshop stands Mr Terrell's orchard. It is plum-picking time, greengage-picking time, time to take honey if you have any hives. The trees round Mr Terrell's buildings are hung with green and golden drops of fruit. Mr Terrell is in his stable: he is at the other end of the process. Embowered in fruitfulness, he is forking out manure. Green cavernous avenues are every way he looks; they are vistas of his years: his life has shadowed him over with a rich green; success, in fact. He would be mindful of its origins at such a time – diligence and dung. So I find him, bright, quiet-smiling. Another is not far behind me. Honey, she wants. Is there any chance of a pound or two by next Saturday? Especially for Saturday, as there is a birthday. Well, his son did say he would take some honey off tomorrow. Two pounds? He will see how the crop turns out. He will do his best for her. She leaves a two-pound jar, hopeful. Mr Terrell puts it with others that have been left.

It does not need much imagination to picture how Mr Terrell forty years ago began planting a four-acre orchard, and now it is a cornucopia. Or perhaps it does; to see how he has persevered to this point, when money has lost its sway and produce is the power. The power in the land, literally; though it was far from so when he planted his first tree, and has been even less so often since. Had he some prevision? No, only an instinct for feeling bed-rock under the ebb and flow, which compelled him forward against the tide. What does need imagination is to see his four-acre field as he first saw it, bare to the sky, windswept and derelict, and the little house standing bleakly.

How many people have gone in for market gardening, for fruit growing, since he took his place, and gone out of it again, capital melted away, and enthusiasm? Mr Terrell never had that preliminary glow of the fireside project, which the disillusioned do not allow as one of the pros of a scheme that has gone so completely con. After all, they had their dream. Mr Terrell never had any capital sum for its pillow. With him it was all piecemeal, perilous; and he knew too much of the business for rosy vision. And yet after all he had, besides skill, the only power on earth that could make four acres keep a man for forty years and rear a family, in a country that has rejoiced in being the world's dumping-ground for food. Nothing but such singleness as is in his smile and look could have been proof against reason, and against mood.

As we pass from the stable to the barn he fingers certain plums, names them, differentiates their flavours; is particular to tell me that those are the real old English greengages. His talk is full of qualities. He planted them all as slips from a single tree. There is no rigid order, the boughs twine wild-looking among one another. They are set too close everybody says. They make an arbour of his pigsties. 'But I expected *some* to die,' he explains. The small capitalist who goes in for the business has a mathematical plan. Mr Terrell, scraping shillings together, has always felt his way. Literally he planted his orchard a few shillingsworth at a time. He grafted and budded young trees. When he could temporarily afford no more he even grew fruit from stones and pips. There are puzzling nameless varieties.

He has two of his acres under the plough. 'Yes, our onions did well: they're up there.' He points to steps leading up to a loft in the barn roof. 'My son laid that floor,' he says, as I mounted to see the onions. They lay spread out over the whole of it, large, sound onions. 'There'll be just enough to let every one of our customers have two pounds.' This is a novel situation, of conferring food – as though the consumer has at last discovered the value of it, which the grower has always known in terms of labour and care; as though he and the consumer at last talk the same language.

I praise the floor as a dry storing place. 'One of my boys is good at working with wood; the other he's clever with iron. It's lucky to think that they are both at home now, and took to the business. I can't do much now: I'm over seventy. I never was very strong.' He moves with a certain stiffness, but one does not notice, seeing only the alertness of his eyes. He looks perhaps sixty, no more.

There is a grinding mill in the barn. In the days when trade was bad, and the sons growing to manhood, the four acres seemed quite inadequate for them, and one boy decided to go to Canada. But then a neighbouring farmer said, 'Look here, I'm giving up my grinding business: if you care to take it on I'll let you have the mill and engine cheap.' So the boy – the one clever with iron – reconsidered his decision, and instead of migrating to Canada bought the mill and set it up in his father's barn.

We are walking round his holding now, through apple avenues. It is not a very scientific holding: he does not spray his trees. Originally the cost was a consideration. He produces saleable fruit, and that satisfies him. But in another way he is less questionably thrifty, that is in planting trees in his boundary hedges. The fruit that overhangs the highway on that account he does not look to gather; that is a sort of bonus to the passer-by. In the same spirit, while he is weighing out the greengages Nora has commissioned me to get, he is insistent that I should help myself from the basket out of which he tips them.

Ah, the sweetness of greengages in their season: it is all the sweetness of summer. I go on eating and spitting out the stones. Old English greengages, thousands of them hanging before my eyes; Mr Terrell in his barn talking of his life, till he forgets what weight of fruit it is we are weighing. Nora meanwhile has gone on to the town to get rubber rings for her preserving jars, has returned and seen my bicycle still standing there, and reached home; and still I am talking and eating greengages. For I am truly at home here, sitting on this bag of grist, my heart is at home. For I have met an English peasant-proprietor, that most honourable, rare, and misunderstood of men. It is fineness, not boorishness, that is his hallmark. A feast of English quality it is: this one man's success cancels a host of defeats for me: it is the very sweet and secret juice of England that has come to fruition against the bitterest weather, economic and political, of all time.

And this is his life which he relates to me: it began with a chance word I let fall on grinding, on flour and bread, so to cooking. 'Yes, I understand about baking: I can cook. It was very handy when my wife was having the children. You see, I started work as a baker's apprentice when I was eleven. I used to carry a board on my head. It was long hours in those days.' His father worked for a nurseryman. When rheumatism crippled the father and he could no longer work, his son left the bakery and took on his job in the nursery garden. 'My brother worked there, too. We never earned more than fourteen shillings a week, either of us.

Still, we saved a little somehow; and one day, passing this way on a journey for my master, I saw this little house and field for sale, and it came into my head we might buy it and start on our own. We hadn't got enough money, of course, but we managed to get a mortgage. The house was a double-tenement then. I got married and lived in one end, and he had the other. But after a while he went abroad. Those were difficult times: the children came quickly. Often I didn't know which way to turn for a sixpence.'

The picture is clear as he talks of those days – winter, snow clogging under the horse's hooves as he drove his van to a town fifteen miles away to sell his goods, so that he had to get down every mile or two in the bitter wind. A poor trade when he got there, then the slow drive home in the dark to the infant family in the little house. Yet always he fought to keep out of debt. He even delayed ordering his seeds till he had the money. The firm he dealt with once wrote inquiring for his order. He answered, telling them why he had not given it. They offered him credit, gladly. One year he had a bit of luck with pigs; bought a sow going cheap in the market, and she turned out to be a good breeder. He sold a batch of pigs for fifty pounds. Fifty pounds: it was wealth; but it went to pay off the mortgage. The house and acres were his own untrammelled property, but still he had no ready money. It was like starting all over again. To get his land ploughed he had to hire. Of course, the plough came when the weather was such that it often did more harm than good. Eventually he sank what little money he had again accumulated in a small mechanical plough. It soon went wrong. He had it repaired, price seven pounds. He had been up and down the field half a dozen times with it, after getting it back from the repairer, when it literally blew up. 'I was glad to be quit of it. I turned to my horse: I understand a horse. I bought a one-horse plough: but it was too heavy for one horse to pull on this land. Then my eldest boy who was growing up said, "I'll make you a little plough, Dad, just right for Tommy." I laughed, not thinking he could do it. But he worked away with all sorts of odd bits of iron; and there is the plough that he turned out.'

It is a neat thing: Mr Terrell points out its component parts, which have half a dozen different sources, some of them domestic. But it works. Later, the same son made a miniature rib-roller out of worn convex plates of his grinding mill clamped together. Next came a horse hoe – I believe there was part of a bedstead in that; then a harrow. Now there is a complete set of miniature farm implements for the two arable acres. The other son has his bees: he maintains the barn and buildings.

What a force of faith and ingenuity has gone to the sustaining of those few acres. I marvelled aloud. Mr Terrell explained, 'Of course, I've always loved the work. However hard I'd worked all day, if there was just a glimmering of light left, I would walk round the place last thing. I loved to see the things growing.'

Well, there is the explanation; a dogged sort of love – single to the exclusion even of business sharpness ('I've not liked to charge poor people so much') – creative, re-creative. For after all how should Mr Terrell look sixty, who is over seventy and was not strong in the beginning? Whence the ever-present smile? Another, who had the business instinct, has travelled the world, made money and lost money, while this man has been watching things grow in the last glimmerings of days. Now, at last, he has come into his own (does his brother call him lucky?) nationally and economically: the whole of England acknowledges him, the primary producer. But he never speculated on that chance, living his quiet destiny.

This has cheered me. That a man has only to be certain in himself to do what he will. This I have felt – but dimly, waveringly. Now it is proved to my sight. For of all impossibilities, to one who knows something of farming, to buy four acres without any capital, and then proceed to make it support you and a family for forty years is the most impossible.

TEN

Harvest festival

FOR SOME REASON, when we were shocking up the beans this afternoon, I thought of an elderly schoolmaster I met years ago at a friend's house. He had recently retired, and was having a house built. It had proved to be more perplexing than he had imagined. Only that day he had received an assortment of door handles to choose from. He was feeling a bit engulfed by all these details as we walked round my friend's garden after tea. The fields were ripening, and I spoke of the harvest at hand. Immediately his eyes brightened, and he told me of how in 1917 he and a party of his pupils had spent the summer holiday helping with the harvest on a Yorkshire farm. How they had worked and eaten and slept! He continued to dwell upon it for the rest of the time I was with him; and when we said goodbye he stood taller, younger: that harvest holiday had been a great event in his life. There had been nothing quite like it before or since; I could see that by the way it kindled him to tell of it, escaping from the door handles.

And yet, superficially, what is there in it? Here we are, trudging round a field that is none too dry, picking up harsh bean sheaves that scratch our arms, grasping a thistle three times out of five, till the fingertips are tender. But yet who would miss it? Who would see a harvest go by and have no hand in it? That is the feeling of young and old; not just those in the position of the retired schoolmaster, to whom it is a novel change, but old men who have toiled with scythe and sickle in their day, as well as the boys who stand expectant round the corn here armed with sticks.

Why should Mr Winch come? He has earned his ease. Yet how he can sympathise by a murmured word, as Jack Ridgewell speaks of his old father now confined to his bed and basket chair. 'He finds the time hang so. You see, when he had his strength he would think nothing of walking seven miles after he'd finished work and had his tea, to cut up a pig he had killed the day before. He could have put the horse in the trap, but he wouldn't bother, he'd just as lief walk. As long as he had a pipe of bacca he didn't mind whether it rained or blew.'

He had been, after all, a man of winds; a miller, a dresser of corn, and of his own millstones, too. 'He'd tap away all day and all night, to get the job done, and come in with blood all over his arms.' The minute punctures of flying fragments of stone were the cause.

Right away back in the windmill we are now: but here we are in the beanfield, too, taking just so many rows of sheaves to a shock. The field curves into a corner of the wood: we come to a narrow end. 'Now, let's see – best put five rows to a shock here, or we shall be left with just two. Then up there' (where the binder stands in some trouble) 'we can take four again.'

Yes, we are very much in the present. 'Look at that cloud boiling up.'

'What are you chaps looking for; lost your gold watch?' Two are searching about at the edge of the wood. 'No, we were just seeing what a lot of nuts there are this year.'

'Ah —' Jack stares over the stirring mass of the standing wheat ('Yeoman?' 'No,' says Mr Camm, 'It's got a curious name – I've forgotten – but bred from Yeoman'). 'I don't like to see the wind draw water into the sun.'

There is a stopping place by the gate; again and again we come round to it. The place where bottles of tea lie in the grass, where the small square tin is brought out and shag laid nicely along the cigarette paper, coaxed with the forefinger.

'How are your arms? They feel it a bit till they get hard.'

It is only the beginning of harvest, and the arms are tender yet, embracing sheaves of sharp straw.

'Old Boley – d'you remember old Boley?' (the tongue sliding along the cigarette paper). 'I never did see him with a pair of gloves on; and there were some thistles on that farm then. His hands were like leather. Why, he'd hedge all winter with his bare hands, too.'

The binder is still in trouble: a bean gets under the canvas where an inch of it is torn and stops everything. Is it moving again?

'One day, when Mr Greaves had High Farm, I came into the field and he called to me, "Just come here a minute." The men were shocking up wheat at the far side of the fifteen-acre. "Tell me, Jack, which way are those men moving?"

'I looked for a bit, and then I told him, "They're moving downhill."

'"Thank you," he said. "That's all right, they're good steady chaps. I don't like to be a spuffler."

'He would come to you and say, "Don't plough too deep, two or three inches, that's plenty." He'd make a man take a log off the harrows. "Give the horses plenty of corn," he'd say.

'Of course,' Jack added in explanation of such a paradoxical farmer, 'he had plenty of money.'

So we go round and round the field and unwind the years. Jack and I happen to be next to each other: we meet with a sheaf under each arm, stand sheaf to sheaf, and part again, stooping after more.

'My father used to kill a pig a week at home. I used to help hold the pig. One day I kept quiet till he'd done, then I said, "I'm going right in now."

'"Why, what for?"

'"That pig bit my thumbnail off."

'My father: no weather never hurt him. He only had the doctor once, for a cold that he took no notice of and it took hold of him inside. "Why aren't you in bed?" the doctor said as soon as he see him. He gave him a bottle of medicine. He only took one drink of it. "Ugh – fetch me some beer." He wouldn't go to bed. I see him rolling about on the green by the mill in pain; but he went on taking corn and meal about in the cart; till gradually he got the better of it.'

The young boys are whittling at their sticks with pocket knives, waiting for the rabbits; country boys and evacuees.

It is certainly going to rain; but we are close behind the binder with our shocking of the sheaves. There is a power of rest in the midst of labour which these men have. Though the arms are tender now, and the fingertips; and the feet tired with walking round and round the field of sticky earth; yet the eyes are bright with the re-created years. The mind reposes on the ample traditions of use, of custom, and of men who knew the need to do the same things in the same sort of way. Of weather that behaved thus and thus; of weather whose freaks, remembered, set a limit to the worst that that oncoming cloud may do. A sort of rainbow of the unwritten covenant, assuring us that we *shall* bring all this corn in safe at last.

'When the wheat was damp my father used to grind a little maize with it: that would clear the stones.'

'Another thing, sacks and sacks of acorns my father used to grind. Wonderful grub to fat pigs on. They used to send the kids out gathering them in the woods; it didn't take them long to collect a bushel. Everybody had a pig fatted on acorns and a little barley meal.'

'Yes, we always did our own bacon. Wet days we'd have a whole day at home doing the bacon, or baking bread and cakes.'

'I wouldn't have any but stone-ground flour. My father he wouldn't eat any other.'

'But what's the difference? Isn't it just a matter of how much is dressed out of the flour afterwards?' I ask.

'No. Roller mills only crush the grain, the stones work contrary to each other; they grind it. There's a lot of difference. Try fatting pigs on meal from a roller mill and then on stone-ground. They'll do twice as well on the stone-ground: it's more digestible.'

We shell out some of the beans we are shocking. They are a good crop: we hold them in our palms. 'They will fat cattle, same as they used to, as I can remember.

'The taters look well, too. The biggest crop of taters I ever saw was grown with fish manure. Truck loads of cods' heads and innards came to the station. How they stank. The men could hardly bear to unload 'em. They made a heap of them in the field. The rats that ran about there! Master great old rats: people got so they hardly dare go that way at night. At last it was all spread and ploughed in and the taters set. We lifted tons and tons off that field, the biggest taters I ever see – and every tater tasted of fish.

'Yes, that's truth I'm telling you. You couldn't eat 'em; not except you were eating fish, too.'

'These Fen taters, too; they're big and beautiful to look at – but no flavour.'

So, there's no easy way out, no short cut to fertility and flavour. But turnings of dunghills, slow composting of decays . . .

This is what harvest is: hard, hard labour of body, but also a stamping of the feet upon the great bedrock of tradition.

It has started to rain. Mr Camm is hurrying off with the binder canvas under his arm, to get his wife to sew it. It all comes back to the woman then, and her needle and thread, to get the harvest on.

I am leaning on the gate, and suddenly it is as though I had all day to do that and nothing else, or anything else; to stare at butterflies, at clouds. But it is not so; it is the attitude of leaning on the gate, familiar and easy, that induces the idle mood, looking out upon the passing world. The passing world at the moment is represented by nothing more lively than a strip of road and a field of indifferent barley beyond. Just outside the gate stand Nora and Anthea waiting for the bus. Martin and Sylvia and I are on the inside waiting to see them off. They are calling all sorts of messages through the bars, while I try to remember things needed from the market town, but this idle leaning on the gate has put them all out of my mind.

The bus arrives with half the village already packed into it. We receive a general smile, and our wave to our two becomes in return a general send-off. Small journeys become big ones by reason of their fewness, and something of an ancient 'God-keep-you' follows them from me, as they go forth into the dangerous hours of today.

The twins go dancing away from the gate across the meadow on a game of their own, and I must set to work. There has been rain: the weather, now black, now brilliant, holds up the harvest. It is the twins' birthday tomorrow. There is a bed of roses in front of the house smothered in weeds, and the grass ankle-deep around it. There has been no time to touch it. But this morning I think that by working furiously I could get that looking trim by dinnertime as a contribution to the birthday. I am worried by a shortage of food for the growing chickens. I set to work with a fork, turning over the bed, and wondering what to feed my birds on. They are at the hungry stage of growth, and there is no corn for them to glean yet. But the sight of sour earth turning over fresh and dark is a never-failing pleasure, and I forget to worry. Suddenly I am aware of a moving mass at my feet, almost on the prongs of my fork. It is the chickens: they have seen me or smelt the earth, and are through the hedge and round it and over it, and are gobbling, pecking, squawking, tugging, fighting. Some are feasting on ants and ant eggs, bringing their beaks down like little picks, others are straining to swallow large worms whole. It is as though we were to swallow boa constrictors. After each morsel has been accommodated inch by inch, and the beak finally shut down on the last of it, there is a thoughtful pause, the wide eye is vivid with some inward crisis of capacity. But only for a minute: the internal problem is solved; the chicken rushes again almost upon the points of my fork in eagerness for more. They snatch worms from under rolling clods that are boulders three times their size, and deftly escape the falling weight. My work is clogged; I am mobbed by them – but how they are being fed! I would almost go without my own dinner to see them gobbling and gulping so, their flimsy war diet being reinforced with vast quantities of meat. How beautiful the roses look now against the dark earth, shining clear, like colour lit up out of night. I cut the grass all round, which is not grass, ours not being a proper lawn, but a mass of wild white clover. The right lawn, though, for a smallholder, equal to having a patch of lucerne. Selina soon has her nose buried in a heap of it.

That such a feast of protein should be a by-product of an hour stolen for quite useless beautifying. The fact of the twins being three years old becomes a feast for all.

So Sunday comes, that is the birthday. A fine day. No, I insist I will not do a thing more than feed and milk today, in spite of many temptations to small tasks. Some are never happy without employment for their hands: for myself, I like to be idle or hard at work. If idle, then positively idle. In hard work there is also a repose. It comes as a gift. Sunday is the fount of it: one acquires a reservoir of it by observing Sunday as a day of rest, and it lasts one through the week. Yes, there was wisdom in the dispensations of our forefathers.

The birthday was memorable for bubbles and candles. Penny bubble pipes were the favourite presents: there was a consolation one for Anthea, too. By nightfall two out of the three were broken; but it had been a glorious bubble, that birthday. A dish of soap and water was soon consumed: Martin imbibed quantities through holding his pipe at the wrong angle. When the other two had mastered the art of swelling out a bubble with gentle breath, he was still puffing furiously through his, expecting to see an enormous bubble appear at once. Then he, too, got the knack, and soon bubbles were floating about in the sun all around them. So great was the bubble enthusiasm that I was only allowed the loan of a pipe for the time it took to blow one bubble, and that not a very good one. Then Martin dropped his pipe and it broke; but he went on blowing at the stemless bowl, assimilating even more soapy water than before. He still had a good appetite for dinner.

There were bats and balls for the afternoon. 'I'm going to keep my ball for ever and ever,' cried Anthea, and next minute lost it. My sitting down under a tree for a rest turned the game of the balls into one of Aunt Sally – at me. While I fended off one, another would catch me a stinging blow on the ear, till I had to get up and go out for a ride in self-defence.

I passed many fine homes, cottage and farm and hall, riding that little way; and heard children calling to one another, and saw women walking out in the sun with their babies; and I thought, there is no land more beautiful, more powerful for good – not with armies – than England.

Here it is flat, but a blue veil of air hangs over the distance that is more mysterious than heights, and a new stack stands like a small bright ark upon it. It has the effect of beauty in a chosen setting, though it all came about by work and daily need.

So, turning in at my own place again, I saw it from the outside, and how the many miles I had walked – and hours worked – between field and field, had composed that picture. Indoors, looking out upon the rose bed I had cleared, now all bloom, the children were sitting down to their birthday tea. I hastened in, with a handful of those green and scarlet balls gathered from wild briars, just in time to see the six candles flaming. They hardly lasted longer than matches, but it was enough, the birthday was commemorated. They had talked so long about those candles, how many would there be, of what colour? It was candles even more than cake they were looking forward to. Now we all blow – puff, puff, puff – out they go, and the sugar roses that are their holders are distributed and eaten.

After tea, songs. Anthea is growing up. 'I'm getting tired of "Hush-a-Bye Baby".' But it is the twins' birthday, so they have their choice, followed by 'Greensleeves' and 'Barbara Allen' for Anthea. And so to bed, hugging their presents.

Before Anthea set out in the bus yesterday to buy the presents, I had the task of extracting pennies from her red money box with the aid of a knife. It took me a quarter of an hour to get ninepence. Her presents to the twins were two similar red money boxes; so in days to come my task of the knife will be trebled.

The twins are having a wild game on their bed, while Anthea is having her bath. Plenty of baths tonight owing to the rain. At six o'clock these summer mornings there is a slight sound which only we parents recognise. It is the creak of bed springs. The twins are jumping about pretending to be goats leaping in the air, or penning themselves in the frame of a stool after taking the top off. I have to get up and send them back to bed – till my back is turned. It is our signal to get up.

Tonight the same game is on. It is all animals with them. At tea I coughed. 'Father did nearly bark,' Sylvia said.

Anthea is full of an idea for tomorrow. In the town she saw some pottery from a local clay. 'One day we are going to where they make those things and I'll get some clay and be able to make jugs and basins for us to use.'

'You'll have to bake them.'

'I'll bake them in the oven. Tomorrow I'm going to start to make some with my plasticine so I'll know the shapes to do them when I get the clay.'

She runs off to the bedroom. In there they are strangely silent. When Nora and I go in they are all sitting side by side making motions with their hands.

'We're having a lovely feast,' Anthea cries; and they continue passing delicious nothings to one another.

Monday afternoon: it is time to eat fourses cake. The barley stack is roof-high, and Jack Ridgewell who builds it goes round it critically before sitting down to food and drink. There is a place for him on the stack cloth which, half unrolled, makes a sort of couch, with rolls of it at either end for bolsters. On this we recline, leaning back on one elbow. The grass is green with aftermath, the stack white, and over the hedge are the summer-baked red tiles of Mr Camm's buildings. There is no road within half a mile: all around us are woods. It makes a classic meal, a banquet of bread, this reclining after labour. And the talk happens to be, as it might have been in Virgil's day, of goats. For one of the young labourers, commenting on our two which he passes daily, says, 'I've drunk gallons of goat's milk; I would now if I could get it. My father used to keep three on the common. Butter and cheese, too, we made: it was lovely.' This though he milks eight of Mr Camm's cows daily, and you might think would be glad to forget the subject. He enumerates all the ways in which he considers goat's milk to be superior to cow's milk. 'It's richer and lighter and sweeter. I suppose you'll not be wanting to part with that kid of yours?'

Others take up the tale; of the commons that here have been so much part of the cottager's life, and are becoming so again now. Of a certain pugnacious billy which attacked all it met, till a well-aimed blow by Jack Ridgewell felled it one day, and the owner came running out very upset. 'You've killed him,' he cried. Jack was quite unrepentant, and a further fight seemed impending. But at that moment the billy opened its eyes, and got up and stood meekly. Nor did it attack anybody again.

Which led us to pugnacious rams, and a particular ram, a champion of pugnacity; and how old Walker, now dead, was charged by it when ditching. He could not move quickly enough to get away, so he faced it with his spade which he levelled at its head. The one who tells this story holds out a big slice of bread to illustrate the spade. He shows with his other hand how the charging ram met it: the fingers divide about the spade of bread. 'That cleft his skull clean in half.'

'You've gone and killed my best ram,' his master complained.

'I can't help that; I only held my spade up; he killed hisself. Don't, he'd have killed me.'

As we resume work I see in the distance a procession of children. Three are mine, one is Ada's: Ada and Nora follow, laden.

It is a gleaning picnic, an idea of Ada's with which to follow up the birthday, hailed with delight. They make their way into Mr Camm's wheat stubble. I saw in the daily press the other day a picture 'by our own cameraman' of people gleaning – among shocks of corn. An unheard of thing – but presumably the picture went down all right. In fact, not only must the corn be carted, but the field raked before gleaning can begin. It is a concession (a tacit one) that our family can go gleaning in Mr Camm's field while the rakings have yet to be carted.

While waiting for a load I go over and talk to them. Gleaning is a kind of diligent indolence: there is no end to it. You do not seem to be working; but strolling, meditating, glancing at the view. Yet in comparatively little time you have a sheaf of corn; corn which would otherwise be wasted, for these fields are too near the wood and its foxes to be safe for fowls, even by day. Seeing the gleaners at it I realised for the first time what a quantity of corn is left even after the modern binder and rake have been over the field. The ears are by no means easy to see among the stubble; the eyes must follow every straw to its end to see if an ear is attached. There are booby traps for the beginner; you see a whole heap of ears and stoop eagerly to shovel them up with both hands, only to find they are empty. They are those that the birds have pecked off when the corn was still standing, and dropped upon the ground to feast on them there. What restraint is necessary, too, to go picking up a straw at a time, when whole heaps of rakings lie there to hand. One realises, as no one who has not gleaned can ever do, what it meant to Ruth that Boaz told his young men to drop some ears out of the sheaves for her to pick up. The word gleaning has come to have a wrong shade of meaning, in the sense of picking up beggarly remnants; but actually some of the fattest ears are among the gleanings.

It is a little festival of the fields. The whole village is out at it. Mr and Mrs Barron are in the next field; they have been there all afternoon, slowly and persistently peering, bending, stretching. They are so intent on their task that, after beginning side by side, they part and nearly meet again a number of times without being aware of each other, following the erratic course that one straw after another leads them. They return at intervals to the heap of corn they have gathered, to add to it. They glean holding their bunch of wheat in the right hand, as a duck might be held by the neck. They pick up more and more with the same hand till it can take no more: the left hand is filled in like manner.

At last a daughter calls Mr and Mrs Barron in to tea: they take up a surprisingly big load for so much standing, and carry it home to their orchard acre.

Our family has already settled to tea, the children having gathered what they consider a sufficient gleaning to justify the picnic. Anthea has brought a book, because 'I won't want to be corning all the time'. Ada's boy is also fond of reading, and has his eyes on the book. As soon as Anthea closes it he opens it, and reads avidly all through tea. At least until Nora passes him one of her jam tarts, which is of such excellence that he just sits munching with a smiling stare at the distance. Beside the family is the sheaf of wheat they have gleaned. Nora is kindled by this gleaning, though hers is interrupted many times by young voices claiming attention. 'Mummy, here's a pretty flower.' 'What for is that man with that horse over there?' 'Oh, Mummy, I've a prickly thing in my shoe.'

'If we could come alone together one day,' she says, 'we could gather a lot.'

Mr Camm's tractor is drawing another load of barley to the stack, which now claims me again. Jack is having a hard job to stack it. The corn was laid, and the sheaves are practically shapeless, short, very dry and slippery, and impossible to bind into place. Added to that there are several loads of loose barley at the bottom of the stack, which makes the worst possible foundation for sheaves. 'They ride about on that loose barley: do what you will you can't keep 'em from riding.'

The loads themselves come leaning drunkenly. Once Mr Camm took both hands off the steering wheel of the tractor to make urgent gestures, which the men interpreted, and ran with forks to hold the load propped the rest of the way to the stack.

We are few now, for the young man who loves goat's milk has gone to milk the cows. I hear the ting of milk in pail. The buildings, which have slept silent all afternoon, now wake to life with the mooing of cows, bleating of calves, followed by the high-pitched squeal of pigs sensing food. Even the ducks are roused, and come up out of the pond quacking loudly.

The energy of body, eye, instinct, that Jack has to exercise in keeping this stack right: who could begin to cope with such a thing, not born to it? A school of art could as well teach a man to produce masterpieces as an agricultural college inculcate the power.

The stack is safely completed as far as the roof: he begins to draw it in. The sheaves now come up with a little green in them. He is glad, for the weeds make the sheaves less slippery. They are better sheaves: I can pass them to him butt-end first; I can see which are the butt-ends.

Yes, he could glean two sacks of wheat in a week, he says, if he could choose his field. He knows just the kind of farmer and just the kind of crop most favourable to the gleaner: the kind whose dilapidated horse-rake jumps on the rough stubble and leaves plenty in the furrows.

Seeing the gleaners, having a vista of them from this stack roof all about the fields of the village, I wonder how much corn is being retrieved this year in this parish, which in years past has been lost. And how much that will be in the whole of England; and how much year upon year in the past we as a nation have let rot into our soil again and replaced from abroad, for the want of this pleasant, sociable, and healthy occupation of evenings on the stubbles. The wheat ear lying there, that has escaped all the implements of harvest, has now become a symbol to us all.

Poor William, unloading uphill to me on the roof of the stack – if he takes off his waistcoat he gets the barley awns down his trousers; if he does not he sweats. As his wagonload sinks down between the two stacks there is not a breath of air. At last it is too much: he strips off his waistcoat.

From the barley stack's narrow top we look down on to the roof of a haystack. 'Do you remember how high that stood when we built it?' Only a month or two back: it seems seasons ago.

The sun sets. I see groups of women and children moving slowly from the stubbles with sheaves and baskets. One family has a sackful. They have a dilapidated bath chair, in which the sack is settled and pushed home like a limp convalescent.

My family has gone some time since. Ada follows with her basket on one arm and her little dog on the other, who is so old now that she can only sniff the air of the hedgerow and go to sleep again, where once she rushed eagerly through thorns and briars. Does she remember those days, I wonder, in the whiff of rabbit-smell she had today?

I make my way across the fields, shaking as many of the barley awns as I can out of my shirt first; but they mostly settle round my waist. I gather up the sheaf of gleanings Nora has left for me to take, this one precious sheaf after forking wagonloads, and cut across the stubble homeward. I break off shoots of ground ash as I go, for Sally loves such things, and her affectionate bleat of welcome merits a response. I am laden with the green and the ripe by the time I reach the home meadow. Nora, bless her, has fed the fowls. All I have to do now is to get out my scythe and mow green food for the racks, close the hen house, milk.

I mow in the dew and the sunset: it is a sweet and restful change from pitching sheaves. The sky is covered all over with silvery mackerel clouds. Robins sing an autumnal evening song. My Cobbett's Corn stands up like a giant wheat, its broad nagged leaves streaming in a gust of wind, its silken tassels of the cobs streaming too. It rustles, nearly ripe. It is both fodder and food, cobs for us, plants for the stock.

Anthea, ready for bed, calls from the window, 'Look, there's a harvest field in the sky.' The mackerel clouds have turned to golden sheaves.

As I mow something goes bouncing away from my scythe. It is Anthea's lost ball. Yesterday she said, 'I've asked fairy Rosebud to find it for me.' But it did not appear. 'I asked her too late at night,' she explained; 'She was busy making the sunshine for tomorrow. I'll ask her tonight before I go to bed.'

A light shines from upstairs: it is not quite blackout time. And there, strangest of illusions, is a woman dressing for dinner! Actually it is Nora slipping on an old frock of flowery stuff with which she graces our supper hour. It has done that duty for three years now. I, too, closing the last door of the yard, fling off my corduroys, scattering grain and awns, wash, shave by red sky-glimmer and robin's song. So we sit down to our supper of eggs, beans, salad, Cobbett's Corn, or whatever our place at the moment provides, and for an hour really rest.

Harvest festival: we take our produce to the church. The church stands in the fields, and now the fields fill the church. I swing back the door whose hinges are like plaited iron, stoop under the low Norman arch, close it behind me. The ring of the falling latch echoes, and all is still. The church has become a cornucopia, in the sunny field solitude of this Saturday afternoon. Not only is there cultivated produce, but the wildness of the hedgerow: the font is entwined with bines, with old-man's-beard. It appears as some pillar remnant of the Golden Age up which Nature has climbed. Sheaves of corn stand up like great shields on either side of the chancel: each sheaf has fixed to its middle, just where the sheaf-knot would be, a great green apple. Plumes of green maize flank the altar.

The village women have done it; they have made the jam which stands on the font among the fluff of old-man's-beard; they have baked the loaf that stands bright and solid in the window. Theirs the fancy and skill which modelled that basket of eggs in butter. They also have had the sensibility to arrange all these in such a natural way, and to bring in the wild bines, too, and make them seem to grow here.

The church itself seems to have quickened and flowered and fruited; so that the font and its angels become an allegory, and the pulpit's three-hundred-years-old wood sprouts living green. It has been done in that unselfconscious, almost absent-minded, mood, in which I have seen a labourer fix a knot of ears of wheat above the dairy door as he passed on his way home after the first day of reaping.

The top of the font has sprays of asparagus fern rising from the centre of it, and drooping over like a fountain, among them fuchsia sprays with their drops of red buds seen through the green haze. Tomatoes, apples, stand under this green fountain among the foamy old-man's-beard. There are bunches of flowers and greenstuff from cottage gardens, and eggs of that colour which makes me remember a farmer's daughter carrying them in a basket. It was an afternoon of high summer, and I noticed the bloom of the sun on her arm. You can call it brown, or golden; but that does not describe it. It is the imprint of summer work on the bare flesh, of carrying corn to the hens in the sun, of working cream into butter in the dairy, the colour of the arm of a working farmer's daughter, young, hardy, and yet smooth and rounded as an eggshell.

Farmers' wives and daughters, although they produce all that is needed for sturdy life, are often nowadays no better off than city folk for food, having town bread brought to them, commercial bacon in rashers, commercial flour. But that arm linked round the basket on that particular afternoon I shall always remember; it matched the eggs in curve and smoothness and life-bloom. Such fragments of summer one likes to recall in quiet hours by the light of autumn fires.

There is a hidden meaning in it. I feel it is the germ of all wholeness, this harvest festival. I sit down in a pew, not to think, but just to be among it and in view of that loaf of bread on the window ledge. The windows are not of stained glass, are not even opaque, so instead of stiff figures of saints one has boughs and birds and the motions of the day. I think churches should all have clear windows, and be surrounded by trees allowed to grow naturally; to let the Genius in by every gleam and motion of the air. To let light glance and move upon the floor, the carving, and all the ancient stillness of the place. It glints now on that old bench-end in the choir which is carved in the form of a greedy fox that has put his head inside a pot and cannot get it out again. It searches out the grain of the pulpit's panelling, and the cream-washed wall has happy reflections.

Sitting here one's eye wanders about the lofty interior. The barn-like beams up there affect one with their horizontal strength, then one is beguiled by a corner of shadow-play. Another carving on a bench-end, a little house, much ruder than the fox, proclaims itself of later date, which is a reversal of the usual assessment of phases of a civilisation.

But what my attention returns to is the loaf of bread. It is a good loaf; the crust almost crackles, and it is still further commended by the sun which claims its old relationship with it, bathing it in its true colour. This side-light becomes somehow the focus of the whole church: everything flows to it, and it stands squat and stalwart. So brightly lit, it is the bread of vision, but real bread all the more for that, bold men's bread, kneaded with bare arms. There are visions latent in a loaf of bread, all the more readily revealed by the discipline of baking it, and in the earth by the discipline of tilling it. And in a knot of wood, whose strength defies your axe. There is enough meaning in the ordinary acts of country life to get the soul to heaven.

The church standing in the fields, its windows clear casements – its interior is in no way esoteric, but simple as a barn. It is sprung as truly from this earth as a medieval village-girl Madonna I saw once in a church window. So the sheaves and the fruits and flowers become the adornment: for stained glass and traceries, their living colours and forms. The church stands empty, but for me it is full of life; everything at its best, the bloom of freshness on it, the spirit shining out of it. Now I could imagine some new life of men bursting in, some true festival. The antique synthesis of this place makes a forward vision of it, a vision of the sinews too. There are roots of sugar beet under the lectern. Yesterday I was lifting those roots, knocking them together. At sight of them all the movements of the work come back to me; I feel them in my limbs. The sheaves bring all the movements of shocking and carting them, their bristly touch and rustle. Tomorrow this service will not be just a thanksgiving of the breath, but a thanksgiving of the body, reliving the labour of the harvest among the sheaves with the men who shared it.

Oh let men work in the light, in the air! It is not because we have exhausted the meaning of simple life that we have achieved complexity. When we have discovered all that we can discover, then we shall turn and rediscover. I think there are certain things that are for ever – fragments of the immanent kingdom. There shall always be ears of wheat above our lintel at harvest, always human arms of the tone and texture of summer work. And an ancient church furnished with new sheaves.

These are moments chosen out of the past to remain with us, to vibrate with happiness. I remember a certain fly glinting on a flower, though hosts of them have come and gone; the light of a setting sun on one old apple bough. I remember a nun sitting in the corner of a railway carriage, and how the calm of her face and dress made the ordinary fashion-clothes of a woman traveller seem flamboyant. I foresaw then some form of dress to supersede fashion, just as I have seen, gazing at a white windmill beyond a field of wheat, that the power of wind and water could be harnessed again with new skill by men.

I see these things beyond this war, clear suddenly through the incandescence; and I know it is not a dream or an escape, but an emergence. Here and there I come flashingly on the real England.

Every morning I see this real England reborn, waking in the cool of the morning with dew upon it; the sails stir, the plough and the chisel go forward; every man in his own sanctuary of spirit, holding steadily to the whole through the detail. In every village there is a monument to the skill and faith of the past. This is the power-house of the future, whence men will draw practical vision and integration for what they do. They will rediscover worship. Except for that the whole of humanity would be destroyed. And it will not be destroyed because, for one reason, of the small flame of truth that these village churches have kept alive, so that one with eyes to see *could* see.

In the city the spire of the cathedral is stately as a ship among the clouds, journeying impassively from the past to the future. This is the sign we shall know the future by, when men's works grow out of their lives, not only out of their heads, and their homes are bowers of their lives, budding abundantly. All around, the motley architecture of commerce will pass away. That finger of stone will not pass away.

I entered from the city square through a ray of sun that blinded me at the door, and suddenly was in a soaring fountain of stone. Despite my familiarity with that interior, the shock of surprise was even greater than before. That such a thing can be. One needs no other proof of the past. The realisation of a vast extension of human powers. One has lived so long in this great commercial rat-trap of a world that one forgot that man could arise in freedom.

Yet withal this cathedral is no greater than my village church in the fields, or the hearth of a family at peace.

The family was sitting on the grass, and the swallows in a row above. Our roan calf cropped the aftermath and the pigs were rustling peas out of a forkful of bines I had thrown into their brushwood pen. A late brood of chicks, gawky, were almost daring to peck the bread and butter out of our hands.

'I expect it is the last time we shall have tea in the orchard this year,' I said, as I edged from the lengthening shadow of a tree.

'Oh, but won't there be just *one* time more?' Anthea pleaded.

'Just one time more, perhaps; but look, the swallows and martins are getting ready to go.'

'They go to Africa,' Anthea informed us, twirling on a stick her little globe that is the size of a tennis ball; and her thumb covered the whole extent of their journey. 'They fly all day and all night over the sea. I read about it in my book. They must be *very* tired when they get to Africa.'

'But *our* Martin not go,' cried Sylvia.

'Oh no, he won't fly away,' we laughed. 'He will stay here with us and wait for them to come back in the spring. And one day we shall see them mending their nest again above your window, babies; and in a little while they'll have babies of their own, just as they had this year.'

When the twins were born, and there were all-night vigils over their small uncertain lives, there was a continuous stirring on the other side of the wall. Stirrings and as it were splutterings, very similar to the stirrings and splutterings of the twins in their cradles, never ceasing through the night. Perhaps that was why we called the boy Martin, though we did not do so consciously for that reason. The birds with their burden of parenthood were neighbourly to us; their stirrings were company in the silence of the night. When, later, the young birds took the air, our young lay under the trees waving their arms at the leaves.

Last spring again the parent birds came and mended their nest in the eaves, and soon another assembly of small heads was peeping out.

Looking at them now it is difficult to believe in their accomplishing that vast journey. They seem almost part of the family, who have woven their flight through all our summer work. It is as though some part of us were flying off to Africa. But they will come again, and be as English to us as the May. Meanwhile our land and our children will so occupy us that the months will fly as fast as the swallows till the swallows come again.

EPILOGUE

AND THE YEARS have flown fast too. The swallows and martins have come and gone for twenty years since we sat on the grass having tea between the long September shadows of the orchard on that day. Always they have seemed to be the same swallows, but the family has grown up.

Schooldays arrived. On a day in May we left a small boy waving goodbye to us through a glass door (oh, what a cold May), with a hearty headmaster standing behind him. Soon afterwards, Nora departed with the girls, returning alone the next evening.

'Did you leave them happy?' I asked.

'Yes,' she answered, 'very happy,' turning to put the kettle on, and dropping two tears as she did so, which hissed on the hotplate.

The good times were meeting the school train. The not so good times were the end of the summer holidays, returning from the station to a silent orchard, and a few playthings lying about.

It was 'Goodbye, Fluffy' – 'Fluffy' being the name of the black and white cat ('a Friesian cat' they called him) which companioned the twelve years of their growing from toddlers to undergraduates. It was 'Hullo, Fluffy', as he appeared (which he always seemed to do) round the corner of the house as the car arrived at the door.

There was learning to ride bicycles – the falling in heaps, the bruises, bent pedals, skewed handlebars, even collapse of a front wheel which precipitated Martin into the ditch.

Bicycles became second nature.

There were exam papers brought home. I looked at the questions and realised my children already knew more than I did, as I went my now middle-aged round of the cows and the kale.

There was the evolution from children's party to teenage dance (though there was no such word as 'teenage' yet). There was the first 'grown-up' party frock, that Nora spotted when looking for a frock for herself. 'That would suit Anthea – it's her blue.' Nora tried it on for her daughter, who was the same height as her mother now.

Said the salesgirl, 'If madam would stand naturally it would look better.' Nora before the mirror thrusting herself out behind and before to approximate to the figure of a budding fifteen-year-old.

There was the invitation to a dance at the Big House on the day of return to school. Disappointment bitter. We connived at a 'cold' for Anthea, and sent Sylvia (still too young for adolescent dances) back alone, with a story of a cold. Parents plotting to deceive. Sylvia acted her part so well that the headmistress wrote saying, 'Anthea is not strong: do you not think it might be a good idea to have her inoculated against colds?'

Then came universities. Glamorous (for us) visits to Oxford in Eights Week – the sparkle of early summer and 'a spirit of youth on everything'. Visits to Cambridge – walking between the crocuses on the Backs to dine with our son in his rooms in King's College, to attend candlelit evensong in King's Chapel – and finally to be photographed beside him on the lawn outside the Senate House when he had taken his degree.

And so on, to twenty-first birthdays, to weddings. The family scattering to their own lives ('The sight of a heap of sugar beet always makes me feel nostalgic,' writes Anthea). Visiting daughters in their own homes, tasting meals derived from, but subtly different to, their mother's meals. Periods of grass-widowerhood for me when grandchildren were being born. And so to the swallows' return and babies on the lawn again.

Please contact Little Toller Books
to join our mailing list or for more information
on current and forthcoming titles.

Nature Classics Library

IN THE COUNTRY *Kenneth Allsop*
THE JOURNAL OF A DISAPPOINTED MAN *W.N.P. Barbellion*
THROUGH THE WOODS *H.E. Bates*
APPLE ACRE *Adrian Bell*
MEN AND THE FIELDS *Adrian Bell*
THE MILITARY ORCHID *Jocelyn Brooke*
ISLAND YEARS, ISLAND FARM *Frank Fraser Darling*
SWEET THAMES RUN SOFTLY *Robert Gibbings*
A SHEPHERD'S LIFE *W.H. Hudson*
WILD LIFE IN A SOUTHERN COUNTY *Richard Jefferies*
FOUR HEDGES *Clare Leighton*
LETTERS FROM SKOKHOLM *R.M. Lockley*
THE UNOFFICIAL COUNTRYSIDE *Richard Mabey*
RING OF BRIGHT WATER *Gavin Maxwell*
FRESH WOODS, PASTURES NEW *Ian Niall*
THE SOUTH COUNTRY *Edward Thomas*
SALAR THE SALMON *Henry Williamson*
THE SHINING LEVELS *John Wyatt*

Also Available

THE LOCAL *Edward Ardizzone & Maurice Gorham*
A long-out-of-print celebration of London's pubs
by one of Britain's most-loved illustrators.

LITTLE TOLLER BOOKS
Stanbridge Wimborne Minster Dorset BH21 4JD
Telephone: 01258 840549
ltb@dovecotepress.com
www.dovecotepress.com